STO

**ACPL ITEM
DISCARDED**

3 1833 00135

S0-BVP-307

FEB 1 5 '71

NUMBER 267

THE ENGLISH EXPERIENCE

ITS RECORD IN EARLY PRINTED BOOKS
PUBLISHED IN FACSIMILE

EDWARD MISSELDEN

FREE TRADE
OR THE MEANES
TO MAKE TRADE FLORISH

LONDON 1622

DA CAPO PRESS
THEATRVM ORBIS TERRARVM LTD.
AMSTERDAM 1970 NEW YORK

The publishers acknowledge their gratitude
to the Syndics of Cambridge University Library
for their permission to reproduce
the Library's copy.

(Shelfmark: Dd*.5.15^3(F))

S.T.C. No. 17986
Collation: A-I^8, K^4

Published in 1970 by
Theatrum Orbis Terrarum Ltd.,
O.Z. Voorburgwal 85, Amsterdam

&

Da Capo Press
- a division of Plenum Publishing Corporation -
227 West 17th Street, New York, 10011
Printed in the Netherlands
ISBN 90 221 0267 x

1566633

FREE TRADE.

OR,
THE MEANES TO MAKE TRADE FLORISH.

WHEREIN,

The Caufes of the Decay
of *Trade* in this *Kingdome*,
are difcouered :

And the Remedies alfo to remooue
the fame, are reprefented.

PROPERTIVS,

Nauita de ventis, de tauris narrat arator :
Enumerat miles vulnera, paftor oues.

LONDON,
Printed by *Iohn Legatt*, for *Simon Waterfon*,
dwelling in *Paules* Church-yard
at the Signe of the Crowne.
1 6 2 2.

TO THE
PRINCE.

SIR,

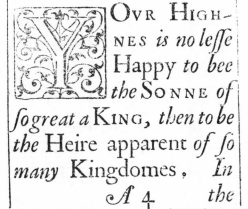

OVR HIGH-
NES *is no leſſe*
Happy *to bee*
the SONNE *of*
ſo great a KING, *then to be*
the Heire apparent *of ſo*
many Kingdomes . *In*
A 4   *the*

the one , *rare endowments of* Maiefty *and* Magnanimity, *are* Yours *by* generation: *In the* other, *a* Royall Monarchy by inheritance and fucceffion. *The* one *doth fit* You *for the* other, *and* Your Royall FATHERS footfteps *for them* both. *In* thofe *are* Peereleffe prints: You *cannot caft* Your Eie, *but they are prefent to* You, *and reprefented in* You. You *fee in* HIS Religion, Piety:

in

in HIS Sacred Perſon,
Tranquility : *in* HIS
Gouernment, Policy. *In
euery* one *of theſe*, all
theſe: and all *in* You. *In
that laſt*, HIS Maieſty
hath carried a quick Eie,
ouer the Commerce *of
this* Kingdome : *becauſe
it hath relation both to
the* Reuenue of the
Crowne, *and the* Com-
mon-wealth *of all* HIS
Kingdomes. *It is ſaid in*
Ezechiels Viſion, *that*
One wheele ran within
the

the other, *which hath an* Empha∫is *in that tongue,* האורפן בתוך האורפן: *and ∫urely matters of* State *and of* Trade, *are involued and wrapt vp together.* Which *latter, becau∫e it is at this time in agitation, and there are, not without cau∫e, many* Quære's *about the* Cau∫es *of the generall decay thereof;* hath cau∫ed *me to put my ∫elfe on this* Enquiry, *to* philo∫ophize *if I could, in the∫e* Cau∫es *and* Remedies. Not that

that *I would seeme with* Phormio, *to reade a Lecture to* Hannibal : *No, Ihaue only* muſtered *and* marſhalled *theſe* men *into their* Rancks *and* Order ; *it is* Yours *to* Command them. *Great* Philip *of* Macedon, *ſuffered a meane muſition to ſay vnto him ,* Abſit, vt hæc tu me melius ſcias. *But for my part , I dare not in any thing, put* ſuch *an* abſit, *to a* PRINCE ſo abſolute. *Euery thing mooues it ſelfe*

to

TO THE

to its Center. *These little lucubrations present them-selues to your* HIGHNES, *as vnto their proper* Orb. *For as they* looke *vp to the* KING, *or as they* looke downe *to the* Kingdome; *In both they* looke on YOV, *with a double aspect.* YOV *are the* Ioy *of the* KING, *the* Hope *of all these* Kingdomes. *The* Only Sonne YOV *are, of the* Only KING: *An hap-py* *SEER, *of a blessed* SIRE: *A* Princely CONSVL,

Ex רָאָה *
prospexit, pro-uidit, quasi porrò-vidit.

CONSVL, *of* the Priuy Councel: A watchman, A worthy, *of* DAVID *and of* IACOB.

These Meditations of mine, *are very* meane: *an vnfit obiect for a* Princes *fight: vnlesse as* YOV *are* a God *on* Earth; *in this also* YOV *reprefent* the GOD *of* Heauen; *to accept in your* Princely *pardon and patience*, τὸ θέλειν ἀντὶ τȣ ἐνεργεῖν. *The* Caufe *is great, your* Wifedom's *deep, and my* Lord the KING

is

is as an Angell of GOD.
YOV *are* HIS, HE *is*
* CHRIST, *and* CHRIST
is GODS.

Oh GOD, *be thou still
the* KING *and* CHRIST,
of this CHRIST Our
KING: Euangelize *vnto
this* Angel : *double the
Spirit of Our* ELIAH, *on
Our* ELISHA : *that* HE
may flourish like our Palme
Tree, *and grow vp like
our* Cedar of * Albion.
Giue thy Iudgements *to
the* KING, *and thy* Iustice
to

Not ὁ χειϲὸς, but χειϲὸς and χρηϲὸς too.

Libanon per Litterarum Metathesin, Albion.

to the KINGS SONNE:
And let all the People
offer these sweete Odours
to Thee *the* God of Heauen, *and pray for the life*
of the KING *and* HIS
SONNE.

So prayeth, for HIs Maiestie,
And your Highnesse,

Ἀνυποκειτῶς,

EDW. MISSELDEN,

Merchant.

From my House at *Hackney*
on *Whitson Eue,* the 8. of
Iune In the yeare of *Grace,*
M DC. XXII. And of the
KING of *Peace,* XX. LV.

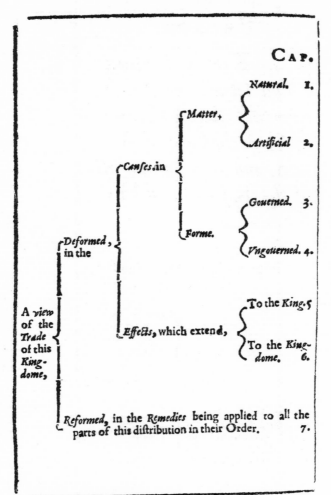

CAP.

Natural.   1.

Matter,

Artificial   2.

Causes in

Governed.   3.

Forme.

Vngouerned. 4.

Deformed,
in the

To the King. 5

Effects, which extend,

To the King-
dome.   6.

A view
of the
Trade
of this
King-
dome,

Reformed, in the Remedies being applied to all the
parts of this distribution in their Order.   7.

CAP. I.

The Caufes of the want of *Money* in *England.*

IT hauing pleafed *God* to giue mee my *birth* and be-ing in this *good Land,* and vnder the *reigne* of fo great a *King*; whofe *peace* and *piety,* whofe *prudence* and *policy,* whofe rare en-dowments of *Nature* and *literature, abfit omnis adulatio,* doe lend

B   to

to the *Christian* and *Pagan* world
such a *glorious luftre*, as that the o-
ther *great lights* in the *spheares*
thereof do feeme *eclipfed* : I could
not but thinke it my bounden du-
ty, in all humble acknowledgement
to *Almighty God*, and deuoted
feruice to fo *mighty a* KING, to en-
deuour to expreffe the fame, in
fome *publique feruice* for the *publique good.*

    The rather for that there feem's
to be a neceffitie impofed vpon all
men, as much as they can, to performe this duety; according to
that generall precept, *Feare God,
Honour the King:* As if a man could
not *feare God,* vnleffe he *honour the
King :* nor *honour the King*, without the *feare of God.*

    And no maruell, when *God* him-
felfe fetteth thefe duties in the
frontifpice or top of both the Ta-
bles of the *Decalogue :* The one
Explicit in the firft Table, *Thou
fhalt*

τὸν θεὸν εὐβεῖσθε.
τὸν βασιλέα
τιμᾶτε.

shalt loue the Lord thy God : The o-
ther *Implicit* in the second Table,
Thou shalt honour the King : as if he
were Νόμος and δ᾽ δ᾽τερος νόμος, *A Law*
& another Law : yea the *whole Law*
comprised in these *two* : and these
two termed the *great Commande-*
ments, to giue a deepe *impression*
and a liuely *expression* of so great a
dutie.

πρώτη καὶ μεγα-
λη ἐντολή; Δευτέ-
ρα δὲ ὁμοία αὐτῇ.

   Yea, he doth honour *kings* with
his owne *title*, as if hee would *part*
with, & *impart* tothem, some of his
owne *honour*. *I haue saide yee are*
Gods : to which that of the *Poet*
may seeme ἀναλογικῶς to haue an ele-
gant allusion, *Diuisum imperium*
cum Ioue Cæsar habet.

In vita Virg.

   And this is it I confesse that hath
raised and *rowsed* mine *affections*,
to seeke out a *subiect*, wherein I
might set my self a task, & as it is in
the *prouerb*, might πανταπάσιν κινειν, to
performe some acceptable seruice,
to so *great a King*, & so *good a king-*
dome.   B 2   But

But what need I *seeke* that which *seeketh* all men? For what is at this time more enquired after then the *Causes* of the *decay of Trade?* And what can be more fit for my *meditation*, then that wherein I haue had *education?* And what hath more *relation* to matter of *State*, then *Commerce* of Merchants? For when *Trade flourisheth*, the *Kings reuenue is augmented*, *Lands and Rents improoued*, *Nauigation is encreased*, *the poore employed.* But if *Trade* decay, *all these* decline with it. Neuerthelesse when I looke vpon the *face* of the *great body politique* of this *weale publique*, and therein consider the *high wisedome* of HIS *sacred Maiestie*, as the *intellectuall part* of this *Microcosme*, or *alter orbis* as *Cæsar* calles it: the *prudence* and *prouidence* of HIS *Nobles*, as the *Eyes* thereof; the great decay of *Trade*, the *Nerues* therof: together with the *parliamentation*
and

and *consultation* of all the *parts*
together about thefe *Caufes* and
Remedies : I feare I fhall feeme
τὸ φῶς ἡλίῳ δανείζειν, to light a Candle in
the Sunne, to offer my feruice in
that, about which the choiceft *wits*
of the *Kingdome* are now in *conful-
tation.*

But hauing had experience of
H I s *Maiefties* gracious interpreta-
tion of fmall *feruices* of his fubiects
employed for the *publique*: though
others much more fufficient are
fent before, yet could I not but ex-
poftulate with my felfe , what if I
alfo *runne after,* and caft in my λεπτὰ α᾽
δύο, into this great *Treafury.*

Therfore if herein, any *obferuati-
ons* of mine, either *Forrein or domeftique* , may adminifter any thing
worthy the *information* of that
Great common and yet not common
Senfe, I fhall efteeme my part moft
happily acted, to haue employed
my *priuate paines* for the *publique*
B 3 good.

good. The rather, for that, as there are many *Caufes difcuffed* and *difcourfed* of at this time, of the *decay of Trade* ; fo alfo are there many *remedies :* wherein if either the *Caufes* be miftaken, or the *remedies* ill applied ; the prefent ficknefle of the *Trade,* may be brought from a difeafe in *fieri* to an *habituated* and in *facto,* as the *Phifitians Schoole* hath it.

    To find out the *Caufes* of things, is a worke of *Philofophy,* and much *felicitie :* to finde out a fit *remedy,* is of high *eminency :* But to apply the *remedy,* is a matter of *State* and *Policy.* And this leadeth mee to the *Method* of my *difcourfe :* which parts it felfe in twaine : *viz.* Into a *double Quære,* of the *Deformation* and *Reformation* of Trade. In the *former* may be confidered, the *Caufes* and *Effects* thereof. In the *Caufes,* the *matter* and *forme* of Trade. The *matter* of Trade, is either

Felix qui potuit rerum cognofcere caufas. Virg.

The diftribution.

                      Naturall

Naturall or *Artificiall.* The *Natural matter* of *Commerce* is *Merchandize* : which *Merchants* from the end of *Trade* haue ſtiled *Commodities.* The *Artificiall matter* of *Commerce* is *Money* , which hath obtained the title of *ſinewes* of *warre* and of *State.*

   Old Iacob bleſſing his *Grandchildren,* croſt his hands ; and laide his right hand on the *yonger* , and his left hand on the *elder* : And *Money,* though it be in *nature* and *time* after *Merchandize* ; yet foraſmuch as it is now in vſe become the chiefe, I will take leaue of Method, to handle it in the firſt place.

   Firſt therefore for the *want of Money* in this *Kingdome,* many reaſons may bee aſſign'd. Whereof ſome are *Immediate* , ſome *mediate* or remote . The *Immediate* reaſons of the want of money, are either ſuch as *hinder* the
B 4   *Importation* ;

The Immediate cauſe of the want of money in England, is the vnder valuation of his Maieſties Coine, which hindereth the Importation, and cauſeth the exportation thereof.

Importation ; or such as *cause* the
exportation thereof. And *both*
these are occasioned by the *vnder - valuation* of *his Maiesties
Coine*, to that of our Neighbour *Countries.* For who will procure licence in *Spaine* to bring
Realles into *England,* to sell them
here at *ten* in the hundred gaine,
which is lesse then the *Exchange*
from thence will yeeld ; when hee
may haue for the same *fiue and
twenty* in the hundred in *Holland?*
Here fiue *Reals* of eight, which
make *twenty* shillings sterling, will
commonly yeeld *two and twenty*
shillings or thereabouts : and the
same in *Holland* will yeeld *forty
two shillings & sixe pence* Flemish,
which is *fiue and twenty* shillings
sterling. And how can we choose
but want money in *England,* when
the *Iacobus* pieces, are *Currant* at so
high a rate in *Holland?* For there
they goe at *twelue* gilders *eight
                                stiuers*

Spanish Re-
als worth 1 s.
in the C. in
Holland.

ſtiuers the piece, which is *one* and *fortie ſhillings* and *foure pence* Flemiſh, which is *foure* and *twentie ſhillings* & *nine pence* ſterling. And after this rate H I S *Maieſties* other *Coines* of *gold* & *ſiluer* are there of reſpectiue value. For although by the *Placcaets* or *Proclamations* of thoſe parts, the *Iacobus* pieces, and other *ſpecies* of gold and ſiluer, are there ſet at indifferent rates anſwerable to their valuation here with vs reſpectiuely, which they there call *permiſſie gelt, Proclamation money* : yet they haue other deuices to raiſe money, and draw it away at their pleaſures. As either by their *Banckes*, when the *Banckiers* will for their occaſions giue a greater price for mony then the *Proclamation* ſuffereth, & then it is called *Banck gelt* : or elſe by ſlacke paymaſters, that for their owne aduantage in the raiſing of money, will pretend not to make preſent payment

payment of their debts, vnlesse you take their money at a higher rate, then either the *Proclamation*, or the *Banck* money. Which being paid and receiued, produceth a third kinde, which they call *Currant gelt*. And so by the Conniuence of the Magistrate, the same goeth from man to man, and at last becommeth

Three sorts of money in Holland: Permiffion money: Banck money: and Currant money.

currant at an excessiue value. So they haue *Permiffion* or *Proclamation Money*, and *Banck Money*, and *Currant Money*, and all to draw dry the *Currant of* His *Maiesties Coine*.

And thus the *Hepatitis* of this *great Body* of ours being opened, & such profusions of the *life blood* let out; and the *liuer* or fountaine *obstructed*, and weakened, which should succour the same; needes must this *great Body languish*, and at length fall into a *Marasmum*.

I am not ignorant that there hath beene great abuse in the culling of His *Maiesties Coyne* here at home, and

and in melting the heauy money into plate : And that there is a great superfluitie of *Plate* generally in priuate mens hands more then is necessary, and farre beyond any example of former times, which must needes also cause scarcitie of money : yet on the other side I cannot deny, but that it is better to haue the same in *Plate,* as a *treasure* of the *Kingdome* ; then *turned into Coine,* & so *turned out* of the *Kingdome,* by the vnder-value thereof.

Now the *Mediat* or remote reasons of the want of money in *England,* are either *D omestique* or *Forreine.* The *Domestique* are *generall,* or *special.* The *general remote* cause of our want of money, is the *great excesse* of this *Kingdom,* in cõsuming the *Commodities* of *Forreine Countries,* which proue to vs *discommodities,* in hindering vs of so much *treasure,* which otherwise would bee brought in, in lieu of those *toyes.*

The Mediate Causes of the want of money are Domestique or Forreine. The Domestique is generally, Excesse.

toyes. For now a dayes moſt men liue aboue their callings, and promiſcuouſly ſtep forth *Vice verſâ,* into one anothers *Rankes.* The *Countrey mans* Eie is vpon the *Citizen* : the *Citizen* vpon the *Gentleman* : the *Gentleman* vpon the *Nobleman.* And by this meanes wee draw *vnto vs,* and conſume *amongſt vs,* that great abundance of the *Wines* of *Spaine,* of *France,* of the *Rhene,* of the *Leuant,* and of the *Ilands* : the *Raiſins* of *Spaine,* the *Corints* of the *Leuant,* the *Lawnes* and *Cambricks* of *Hannault* and the *Netherlands,* the *Silkes* of *Italie,* the *Sugers* & *Tobaco* of the *Weſt Indies,* the *Spices* of the *Eaſt-Indies* :   All which are of no neceſſitie vnto vs, & yet are *bought* with ready mony, which otherwiſe would be *brought* ouer in treaſure if theſe were not. A *Common-wealth* is like vnto a *family,* the *father* or maſter whereof ought to ſell more then he buyeth, according

according to old *Catoe's* counſell,
*Patrem familias vendacem non ema-
cem eſſe oportet.* Otherwiſe his *ex-
pence* being greater then his *reuenue,* he muſt needs come behind
hand. Euen ſo a *Common-wealth*
that exceſſiuely ſpendeth the *forreine* Commodities deere, and vt-
tereth the *natiue* fewer and cheape,
ſhal enrich other *Common-wealths,*
but begger it ſelfe. Where on the
contrary, if it vented fewer of the
forreine, and more of the *Natiue,*
the reſidue muſt needs returne in
treaſure.

The *ſpeciall remote cauſe* of our
want of money, is the great want
of our *Eaſt-India ſtocke* here at
home. Which is a matter of very
great conſequence, and cauſeth the
body of this *Common-wealth* to be
wounded ſore, through the *ſides*
of many particular members thereof. For the *ſtocke* of the *Eaſt-India
Company* being of great value, and
collected

Νήπιοι ἐδ᾽ ἴσα-
σιν ὅσω πλέον ἥμι-
συ παντός, ἐδ᾽
ὅσον ἐν μαλάχῃ
τε καὶ ἀσφοδέλῳ
μέγ᾽ ὄνειαρ.
Heſiod.

The dome-
ſtique cauſe
in ſpeciall, is
the want of
the *Eaſt-
India ſtocke*
in this *Com-
mon-wealth.*

collected and contracted from all the other particular *Trades* of the *Common-wealth*; and a great part thereof hauing beene *Embargued* and *detained* now for more then fiue yeeres laſt paſt; and that not by a *profeſt Enemie*, againſt whom we might haue beene *warn'd* and *arm'd*, but by a *friend*, a *neighbour*, a *next neighbour*, one obliged to our KING and *Nation* more thē to all the Kings on earth : this loſſe I ſay, is not onely thus vnkind, but is the more intollerable, in that the Common-wealth hath loſt the vſe and employment of the *Stocke* it ſelfe, and all the encreaſe of *Trade* which the ſame might haue produced, in the ſeuerall *Trades* of the *Subiects*, whereby abundance of *treaſure* might haue beene brought into this land in all this time.

It is ſaid of *Beliſarius* that great and famous *Commander* of the *Romanes*, that euen *Rome* it ſelfe owed

Crinitus &
Volater.

to

to him twice her life : and yet at
laſt was ſo vnkinde to *Beliſarius* as
to put out both his eyes, and expoſed him to beg in a little Cottage
built without the gates, where hee
often repeated this ſentence to
thoſe that paſſed by , *Date obolum
Beliſario , quem inuidia , non culpa
cæcauit.* And certainely our *Nation* may challenge as much or more
of theſe *vnkinde friends* , then *Beliſarius* euer did or could of *Rome :*
and they ſhew themſelues no leſſe
vnkinde, to depriue vs of the *light*
and *life* of this *Trade* of ours , and
ſuffer this *Nation* to vſe ſo much
importunitie for their owne.

    Homer reports of *Patroclus*, that   *Hom. Iliad.*
he would needs put on *Achilles ar-
mour* , and ride on *Achilles horſe*,
but *Achilles ſpeare* hee durſt not
touch, and thereby was knowne to
Hector, with whom he fought, not
to be *Achilles*, and ſo loſt his life.
Theſe friends of ours haue ſome-
                      times

times *put on* , fometmie; *put off*, I had almoft faid, *put out* the *Kings colours* : They haue fayled in Hrs fubiects *fhippes* , but that *Haftam fidei* they haue not *vfed*, or a-*bufed* rather ; whereby they haue beene *difcouered* to the *Indians*, not to be the *fubiects* of the *faith's Defender* , as fometimes they would haue *faigned* , though to an euill purpofe.

The *Romanes* were wont to weepe, at the fight of *Cæfars blood* kept in an *handkercher*. *Cæfars fubiects blood* is kept, not in *handkerchiefes* but in *fheetes*, written *within* and *without* , the *memory* wherof maketh the people *mourne*. The *cry* thereof is *gone vp* : the *King* will remember it, the *King of Kings* will auenge it.

Conftantinus the *Great*, the father of *Conftantius*, was wont often to proteft, that he made more account of one *Chriftian* then of *all* his *Coffers*

fers filled with *treasure.* And the Comfort of this *Nation* is, to bee the *subiects* of such a *Soueraigne,* who as *constantly* as euer did *Constantinus,* hath againe and againe profest, *Not to account himselfe more rich or happie, then in the prosperitie of his subiects.*

Thus much of the *Domestique remote causes* of the want of money in *England*: the *forreine causes* follow. Which are either in respect of the *warres in Christendome,* or the *Trades out of Christendome. The warres in Christendome* are *forrcine remote causes* of the want of money, either by *causing* the *exportation,* as the *warres of Christians*: or *hindering* the *importation* thereof, as the *warres of Pirates.* I will take the *warres of Germanie* for an vrgent instance of the former: which haue raised the *Riecks daller* from two Markes *Lubish,* to *twentie* markes *Lubish,* in

C many

In diuers Orations and Proclamations.

The forreine causes of the want of money, are the warres of Christians amongst themselues, or against them by Pirats.

many places of *Germany* : whereby abundance of money is drawne vnto the *Mintes* of *thofe* Countries, from all the other *Mines* and parts of *Chriftendome*.

And for the latter, I will inftance the *warres* of the *Pirats* of *Argier* an d *Tunis*, which hath robbed this Common-wealth of an infinite value : the *crueltie* whereof many feele with *griefe*, others heare with *pittie*, but the *grieuance* remaine's. Needs muft *Chriftendome*, and in it *England*, feele the want of money, when either it is violently intercepted by *Turkifh Pirats*, the Enimies of *God* and *man*; or the inftruments furprifed, as *men*, *fhips*, and *merchandize*, which are the *channels* to conuey it to vs. An *heathenifh policie* it is, or *hellifh* rather, put vpon the *Princes* and *people of Chriftendome* by the *Grand Seignour*, to hold with them an outward forme of *amitie*, and in the meane

A Turkifh policie.

meane time by his vaſſals, vſe a
cunning and couert *hoſtilitie*.

   The other *forreine remote cauſes*
of the want of money, are the
Trades maintained out of *Chriſtendome* to *Turky*, *Perſia* and the *Eaſt-
Indies*. Which trades are maintained for the moſt part with ready
money, yet in a different manner
from the trades of *Chriſtendome*
within it ſelfe. For although the
trades within *Chriſtendome* are
driuen with ready monies, yet
thoſe monies are ſtill *contained* and
continued. within the *bounds* of
Chriſtendome. There is indeede a
fluxus and *refluxus*, a *flood* and *ebbe*
of the monies of *Chriſtendome* traded within it ſelfe : for ſometimes
there is more in one part of *Chriſtendome*, ſometimes there is leſſe
in another, as one Countrey wan-
teth, and another aboundeth : It
commeth and goeth, and whirleth
about the *Circle of Chriſtendome*,

C 2   but

*Or the trades
maintained
out of Chri-
ſtendome
with ready
money.*

but is ſtill contained within the *compaſſe* thereof. But the money that is traded out of *Chriſtendome* into the parts aforeſaid, is continually iſſued out and neuer returneth againe. It is true, thoſe trades tend to an admirable encreaſe of the ſtocke of *Chriſtendome* in wares : which if they were purchaſed with the wares of *Chriſtendome*, according to the true nature of *Commerce*, the benefit were farre more excellent. For *Commercium is quaſi Commutatio mercium*, a change of wares for wares, not money for wares. And it is *Libera commeandi facultas, ab ijs qui merces vltro citroque conuehunt.*

* Or if the *Common-wealth* of *Chriſtendome* were like to that of *Vtopia*, where gold and ſiluer are of leſſe eſteeme then Iron, it were a braue exchange to loſe money to get wares. For the riches of former ages did not conſiſt in *re pecuniaria*

Benvenut.
Strac. de mercatura pars. 1.
Calepin.
* *Aurum & argentum ſic apud ſe habent, vt à nullo pluris æſtimetur quàm rerum ipſarum natura mercatur: quâ quis non videt quàm longè infra ferrum ſunt?*
Vtop. lib. 2.

niariâ but *pecuariâ.* Whence *pecu-*
nia, as *Plinie* affirmeth, was fo called *a pecude, quia pecus fuit pecuniæ*
fundamentum, & antiquitus pecunia
pecudis effigie fignabatur. But when
Immooueable and *Immutable* things
came alfo to be in *Commerce* a-
mongft men, as well as thofe things
which were *mooueable* and fit for
change, then came money in vfe, as
the *rule and fquare* whereby things
might receiue eftimation & value.
Therfore the *Ciuilians* affirme that
Numus eſt ἀπὸ τῶ νόμω dictus, quòd
inſtitutum fit Ciuile. According to
that of *Ariſtotle.* Νόμισμα ἀπὸ τῶ νόμου,
ὅτι ὸ φύσει, ἀλλὰ νόμῳ ἔσι. *Numus non eſt*
à natura fed à lege. And thence
it is that *money* in our tongue is
deriued of *moneta, quafi numi nota.*

Or if there were a *neceffitie* to
to *Chriſtendome* to vfe thofe forreine wares: or that the *meanes*
whereby they are to be procured,
were without the loffe of treafure :

Omnes vete-
rum diuitiæ in
re pecuariâ cõ-
fiftebant.
Guich.
Plin.lib.33.

Lib. 1. ff. de
Contrah.cōt.

Lib. 5. Eth.
cap. 8.

or laftly that the fame tended to the encreafe of the treafure there-of, the exchange were excellent. But firft there is no fuch *necefsitie*: for that's neceffarie to doe a thing without which it cannot be done : And that's neceffarie to the be-ing of a *Common-wealth*, without which it cannot fubfift. But thankes be to *God*, *Chriſtendome* is richly furnifhed within it felfe, with all things fit for life and maintenance: whether we refpect *vitall* vfe, as foode and raiment : or *phyſicall*, as vegetables and minerals : or *politi-call*, as gold, filuer, and infinite va-rietie of merchandize. Nor are thofe wares procured without the *loſſe* of treafure, no nor with *leſſe* treafure. For as thofe wares haue coft leffe in *price*, fince fome late difcoueries ; fo are they encreafed in their *quantities*, by the ample trade of all parts of *Chriſtendome* thither, more then before : and then

Neceſſarium illud dicitur ſine quo fieri non poteſt. Calep.

then who knoweth not that a *leſſe*
quantitie *deare*, and a *greater* quantitie *cheape*, is all one in reſpect of
the value. Nor is the treaſure leſſe-
ned by changing the courſe of
trade into thoſe parts. For the *new*
trades found out, are furniſhed
with a new ſupply of money, and
the *old* neuertheleſſe iſſue out as
much treaſure as before: by reaſon
that the ſame are enlarged and become now as great, *apart*, as heretofore they were, *together*, whē the
new trades were included in the
old. So that now ſo much *more* of
the treaſure of *Chriſtendome* is wa-
ſted, as thoſe *old* and *new* trades are
encreaſed, which is to an infinite
value.

Nor laſtly, is the *treaſure* of *Chri-*
ſtendome encreaſed by thoſe forreine trades, for the more the ſtock
of *Chriſtendome* is thereby encreaſed in *wares*, the more it decreaſeth
in *treaſure* : which the parts of

Chriſtendome muſt needs feele by *Sympathy* and *compaſsion.*

And this, that prudent and poli-tique Emperour *Charles* the fifth perceiued in his time, who vpon a queſtion betwixt the *Spaniards* and *Portugalles* about this matter, the Emperour vſed words to this ef-fect: *You Portugalles for a ſuretie, are Enemies to all Chriſtendome; for you carry nothing out of it but coine, which is hurt to all Countries.*

1ς. Hen. 8.
Hall.

Cap. II.

The Cauſes of the decay of Trade, in the Merchandize of England.

SVch are the *cauſes* of the *matter* of *trade* conſidered in the *want of money,* the *marchandize* follow-eth. *Merchandize* is that naturall matter of *Commerce,* whereby men
buſie

busie themselues in buying and selling, chopping and changing, to
the encrease of Artes, and enriching of *Common-wealths*: according
to that of the *Poet*, ἀγαθὴ δ᾽ ἔρις ἥδε
βροτοῖσι, *Bona lis mortalibus hæc est.* Hesiod.

And to the end there should be
a *Commerce* amongst men, it hath
pleased *God* to inuite as it were, one
Countrey to traffique with another, by the variety of things which
the one hath, and the other hath
not : that so that which is wanting
to the *one*, might be supplied by
the *other*, that all might haue sufficient.

Which thing the very windes
and seas proclaime, in giuing pas-
sage to all nations : the windes
blowing sometimes towards one
Country, sometimes toward another; that so by this diuine iustice,
euery one might be supplyed in
things necessary for life and maintenance.

And

3.4.Na.qu.

And this, *Seneca* thought to be a principall benefit of nature, *Quòd & vento gentes locis diſſipatas miſcuit, & ſua omnia in regiones ita deſcripſit, vt neceſſarium mortalibus eſſet inter ipſos Commerciū. Nature by the benefit of the wind, hath ſo mixed people, diſperſed in diuers places, and ſo diſtributed her gifts in diuers Countries, that there ſhould be a neceſſity of Commerce amongſt men.* Which agreeth with that of *Ariſtotle, Eſt tranſlatio rerum omnium cœpta ab initio, ab eo quod eſt ſecundùm naturam, cùm homines haberent plura qnàm ſufficerent, partim etiam pauciora, negotiatione ſuppleri id quod naturæ deeſt, quo commodè omnibus ſufficiat.*

Ε᾽ςι γάρ ἡ μεταβλητικὴ πάντων ἀρξαμένη, τὸ μὲν ϖρῶτον ἐκ τῶ κατὰ φύσιν, τῶ τὰ μὲν πλείω, τὰ δὲ ἐλάττω τῶν ἱκανῶν ἔχειν τοὺς ἀνθρώπους, μεταβλητικὴν ἀναπλήρωσιν τῆς κατὰ φύσιν αὐταρκείας.

De Repub. lib. I.cap.9.

And that we doe not goe out of the *Chriſtian world* for an example hereof, let vs conſider the ſtate of the *Netherlands,* in what a miſerable caſe thoſe people were, if they receiued not ſupply from all other

other *Nations*. They haue *nothing* of their owne, and yet they seeme to possesse *all things* in the *supply* they receiue from *all the world*.

And surely if any *Kingdome* vnder the Sunne can subsist of it selfe, none hath more cause to *blesse God*, then this *Iland* of ours, which *Almighty God* hath richly adorn'd with variety of all things necessary for mans life and welfare. As with *Corne* and our **Wine: Cattle, Wooll, Cloth, Tynne, Iron, Lead, Saffran, Waxe, Hoppes, Hydes, Tallow, Flaxe, Fowle, Fish*, and many others: whereby, thankes bee to *God*, the people of this Land, haue not onely *sufficient* for their owne maintenance, but doe abundantly *supply* the wants of all other *Nations*.

Now the *Trade* and *Commerce* of this *Kingdome within it selfe*, and *with Forreine Nations*, consisting of so many rich Commodities ; let vs consider them all *ioyntly*, and then

* I meane *Beere* which in forreine parts is of more esteeme then wine. And to vs also in the vse, if there were not abuse, is farre to be preferred.

The decay of the Merchandize of this Kingdome, considered iointly or apart.

then some principall of them *apart.*

Iointly considered, the *causes* of the decay of *Trade* in them, may be said either to be *Deficient* or *Efficient. Deficient,* either in the *generall* want of money in the Kingdome ; or the *particular* want of the *East-India stocke.* I shewed before, what were the causes of the want of mony : & that the disaster vpon the *East-India Trade* is a *remote cause* thereof: but these are *both causes* of the *decay* of *trade.* For *money* is the *vitall spirit* of *trade,* and if the *spirits faile ,* needs must the *body faint.* And as the *body* of *trade* seemeth to be *dead* without the *life* of *money* : so doe also the *members* of the *Common-wealth,* without their *meanes* of *trade.* We say, that an *Artizan* or *workeman,* cannot *worke* without *tooles* or *instruments* : no more can a *Merchant trade without money* or meanes.

And

Iointly considered, the causes of the decay of trade are the want of money, and the East India stocke.

And in the *want* of so great a *stocke*, as is that of the *East-India Company*, the *Body* of this *Commonwealth* hath lost the vse of many of it *principall members*; by whose industry, art, and action the *Commerce* thereof might wonderfully haue beene encrea'st. The losse whereof, to him that is not wilfully blinde, is apparently sensible in the *Drapery* of the *kingdome*, wherby the *poore* are set on worke: and in all the other *trades* of the *kingdome*, whereby the *subiects* are employed: and hath begot that great and generall *dampe* and *deadnesse* in all the trades of the *kingdome*, which we vnhappily feele at this day.

    The *Efficient causes* of the *decay of trade iointly* considered, are either *Vsury*, or *vnnecessary suits in l.w*. In the *former* I am preuented, and my labour spared, by him that wrote a little treatise against *vsury:*
              which

Or Vsury.

Entituled a Tract against vsury, presented to the high Court of Parliament.

which it ſeeme's for *modeſty* he re-
fuſeth to owe : though I could
wiſh, that thoſe that deſerue of the
publique were knowne to the *publique* : leaſt they be ſerued as ſometimes *Batillus* ſerued *Virgil* , and ſo
be forc't too late to proclaime, *Hos
ego verſiculos feci, tulit alter Hono-
res*.

I haue a word onely to adde to
his *Vſury*, that it is not an *Vſury* of
ten in the hundred only, that wrin-
geth this *Common-wealth*, but an
extorſion alſo of 20.30. 40 , nay of
Cento per Cento per Anno , as the
Italians ſpeake, giuen and taken on
pledges and *pawnes* , and that on
poore peoples labours , in *London*
eſpecially : which is a biting *Vſury* indeed , and a fearefull crying
ſinne before *God*.

Of Litigious
Law-ſuits.

Vnneceſſary ſuites of Law are alſo
Efficient cauſes of the decay of
trade. Wherein certainely this
Kingdome exceedeth all other
kingdomes

kingdomes in the world. As the *Iustice* of this *kingdom* is the *Diadem*
of the KING, and doth *stabilire Re-
gis thronum*, and *tribuere cuique
suum* : whereby *men* may giue *Cæsar Cæsar's*, and *meum* and *tuum* one
to another : so is the *Iustice* of the
KING, in the *sacred person of* HIS
Maiestie, amongst other HIS *Royall Vertues*, an *Embleme* and *repre-
tation* of *highest Maiesty* : and it is
an incomparable happinesse of this
kingdome, to haue such a *Malchi-
zedec*, a KING of *Iustice*, a KING of
Peace.

Neither may I forget that *Royall*
testimony hereof, which is worthy to be written in letters of gold,
and thankefully to be remembred
of euery *tongue* and *pen*; whereof
amongst others more worthy, it
was also my happinesse to be *ocula-
tus* and *auritus testis* : when HIS
Maiesty in a *Star-chamber* assembly,
lifting HIS eye toward heauen, and
laying

מלכי־
צדק
מלך
שלם

The Com-
memoration
of a royall
protestation
in the Star-
chamber of
His Maiesties
sinceritie in
Iustice.

laying His hand on His Sonnes head, made such a solemne protestation of His sincerity in *Iustice*, as may serue for a matter of admiration and imitation, to all the Kings on earth. Those that went before, and they that followed after : Those that heard it then, and they that heard of it since ; said it was φωνὴ Θεῦ , ϰ̀ ἐϰ ἀνϑρώπε *Nec vox hominem sonat, ô Deus certè* !

If such then be the *Iustice* of the *King* and the *kingdome*, how is it then that *Trade* is hindered by suits of *Law*? Herein *Columellae's* counsell is remarqueable, *Principi prouidendum est, ne legibus fundata ciuitas, legibus euertatur.* There cannot be too much *Iustice*, there may be too much *Law*. For the vse of *Iustice* is excellent, in conteining men within the bonds of *ciuility* and *honesty* : in preseruing men from *iniurie* : and in maintaining euery mans *right & propriety.*

But

De Re Rustica.

Honestè viuere: Alterum non lædere : Suum cuique tribuere. Iuris præcept.

But the abuſe there-of is a moſt pernitious and dangerous ſurfeit in the *body* of euery *Common-wealth.*

And this is our caſe in this *Weale-publike*; no *Kingdome* hath better *Lawes*: no *kingdome* ſo full fraught with tedious, needleſſe, endleſſe, *ſuits* of *Law.* For now this *Litigandi* κακοθεις is become κακοηθης, and waxeth ſo faſt, and groweth ſo great, that ſuites of *Law* doe ſeeme immortall: time doth en creaſe them, and length of time would not determine them, if the wiſedome of thoſe *Graue Fathers* of the *Law*, did not put an end to the malice of the *Litigants*: as is now worthily obſerued in Chancery, to his honour and memorie that hath ſo happily begun the ſame.

By the groweth and greatneſſe of which ſuites, I ſay, a great number of His Maieſties good and lo-

D ving

uing fubiects are vexed, imprifoned, impoueriſhed and ouerthrowne : and whilſt the *Litigants* ſtriue together, another taketh away the *fiſh*, and as it is in the *Apologue*, leaueth to either of them an empty *ſhell*. And thus mens time and meanes being ſpent in *Law*, which ſhould be employed in *Trade*, trade is neglected, and the *Commonwealth* depriued, of the benefit that might be purchaſed and procured thereby.

And thus much for the *decay of Trade* confidered *ioyntly.* It followeth now to confider them *apart*, in ſome principall parts therof. Which may be reduced, to ſuch as tend to the *Fortification of the Kingdome*, or *Maintenance of Trade.* The *former* are *Ordinance* and *Munition :* the too-too common exportation whereof, hath taught vs wofull experience of an invaluable inconuenience thereby, which

The Decay of trade confidered apart, in the Ordinance and Munition.

1566633

which euery man is fenfible of:
and therefore I neede not *preffe* it :
I wifh it did not *oppreffe* vs.

The *latter*, I will referre to
things effentiall, for the preferuati-
on of mans life, as *Victus* and *Vefti-
tus* : yet fuch of them alfo as doe
aford wondrous variety of Trade,
and may be termed the *Nourceries*
thereof, as the *Fifhing* and *Clothing* of this *Kingdome*. For on
thefe two, all forts of *Trades* and
Tradefmen, haue fome depen-
dance.

The inconuenience in the *former*, is that *Encroaching* of *Strangers*, in *Fifhing* vpon our *Coafts* :
whereby not onely the *bread* is taken out of the fubiects *mouth*, but
that infinite *wealth*, which *God*
hath made *proper* and *peculiar* vnto *Vs*, is become *common* vnto
them. Whereby alfo, their *Nauigation* is wonderfully encrea'ft,
their *Mariners* are multiplied, and

Or in the
Fifhing.

D 2   exceeding

1566833

exceeding great *Trades* maintained into all parts of the Chriſtian
world. And victuals commonly
yeelding ready money, and tolleration of exportation thereof, the
ſame hath redounded to an infinite
enriching of their Countries with
Treaſure, exhauſted out of theſe
Mines of our's.

    I am not ignorant that a learned
man of that ſide, preſſing hard in
a Treatiſe entituled *Mare liberum*,
the Community and freedome of
the *Sea* againſt the *Portugall* Trade
into the *Eaſt Indies*: doth cunning-
ly and obliquely, vnder the couert
termes of *Populi Romani littus*, defend and maintaine, in the fift chapter thereof, their *Fiſhing* vpon our
Coaſts. For thus hee concludeth,
*Nemo igitur poteſt à populo Romano
ad littus maris accedere prohiberi,
& retia ſiccare, & alia facere, quæ
ſemel omnes hominibus in perpetu-
um ſibi licere voluerunt.* And
                   againe,

*Mare liberum.
cap. 5. p. 22.*

againe, *Exteris ius piscandi, vbique immune esse debet.*

Eodem cap. p.28.

To part of which Treatise, there is an answere entituled, *De Dominio Maris*, to which I referre those that desire further satisfaction in this matter. But in my iudgement, which I submit to better iudgement, the Author of *Mare liberum*, though otherwise very learned, strayneth his Arguments for that purpose beyond their strength. For *Ius* is said to be *scriptum*, or *Non scriptum*. And *Non scriptum* is *Consuetudo*. And *Consuetudo non minus est species iuris, quàm ius scriptum*. And by both these, the *proprieties* of the Seas may be proued, to belong to those *Princes* and *Countries*, to which they are next *adiacent*.

De Arte iuris cap. 3.

For *Custome*, the examples of our Neighbor Countries round about vs are frequent. As of *Coeldine, Groeneland, Norway*, and *Frisland*,

D 3   vnder

vnder the *King* of *Denmarke.*
Tunny fishing vnder the *Duke* of
Medina. The *Gulfe of Venice* vnder that *Seignory.* And many o-
thers I might inftance: In all which
there is no liberty of fifhing, but by
fpeciall priuiledge had from thofe
Princes to whô the fame belongeth.
Which being fo, we may wel con-
clude with the *Poet, Cùm ventum
ad verum eſt, fenfus morefque repugnant.*

For the *Law* it felfe, it is not
hard to produce fome of his owne
Authors againſt himfelfe. As the
Emperour Leo : of whom he thus
fpeaketh, *Voluit* ωεἰθυεμ, *hoc eſt, ve-
ſtibula maritima eorum eſſe propria,
qui oram habitarent ; ibique eos ius
piſcandi habere.*

Alfo *Rodericus Suarius,* whofe
teftimony becaufe he was a *Spani-
ard,* he produceth againſt the *Portugals* in the end of his fift Chapter ; whom, if hee had pleafed,
hee

Hor.

*Mare liberum.
p. 25.
Nouella Lec. 56*

hee might also haue cited thus speaking: *Redditus piscariarum consueti, vt est gabella, seu aliud tributum solui consuetum, de his quæ in mari piscatores faciunt, seu à mercatoribus de his quæ emunt aut vendunt, Principibus conceduntur.*

To which I will onely adde that of *Bartolus*, whom the *Ciuilians* call *Iuris Lucernam*, thus speaking: *Vt Insulæ in mari proximè adiacentes, sic & mare ipsum ad Centum vsque milliaria pro territorio districtúque illius regionis cui proximè appropinquat, assignatur.*

The rest that the Author of *Mare liberum* enforceth, of the Community and freedome of the *Sea* to all *Nations*, he vnderstandeth of matters in question, betweene the *Portugals* and those of his *Nation*, concerning their *East India Trade*, and not of their *fishing* vpon our *Coasts*. Which *Question* in my iudgement, being *out of question*,

were

Or in the Clothing.

were better determined by *action*
then *disputation*: It being a *Royalty*
of the KING, and a *Regall priuiledge*
of this *Kingdome*, assigned by *Almighty God*.

From the *Fishing* come wee to
the *Clothing* or *Drapery* of this
Kingdome: the consideration wherof is of very high consequence, and
concerneth both the *Soueraigne*
and the *Subiect*, *Noble* and *Ignoble*;
euen all sorts, and callings and conditions of men in this *Common-
wealth*. For this is said to bee a
Flower of the KINGS *Crowne*, the
Dowry of the *Kingdome*, the chiefe
Reuenue of the KING. This is a
bound to fortifie, and a *bond* to knit
the subiects together in their seue-
rall societies. This is the *Gold* of
our *Ophir*, the *Milke* & *Hony* of our
Canaan, the *Indies* of *England*: and
therefore *desire's* and *deserue's* to be
had in an euerlasting remembrance.

The *Draperies* of this *Kingdome*
are

are termed *Old* and *New.* By the
Old, are vnderſtood *Broad Clothes,*
Bayes and *Kerſies*: By the *New*, *Per-*
petuanoes, *Serges*, *Sayes* , and other
Manufactures of *wooll.*

The *cauſes* then of the *decay* of
trade in theſe *Draperies*, are either
Domeſtique or *Forreine.* The *Do-*
meſtique cauſes, are ſome *Paſt*, ſome
Preſent. *Thoſe Paſt*, are apparent in
the late diſturbance of the Cloth-
trade, which is ſo obuious to euery
man , that I had rather *paſſe by it*,
then *preſſe vpon it*, becauſe it is *paſt*:
and I would to God that ſo were
the effects of it alſo. In charitie
we may thinke it was *good* in the
purpoſe, though it prooued *ill* in the
practiſe. For thereby the *Drape-*
ries of this *Kingdome* are much diminiſhed , and the forreine aduanced and aduantaged. The quantities of which laſt, were formerly few or none, but now they
exceede our higheſt numbers iſſued

ed out of the land: as by a collection thereof, which my felfe made in
thofe parts, by H1 s *Maiefties* fpeciall cõmand, in the time of *Secretary
Winwoods* feruice, may appeare.

Thefe prefent, may be difcern'd in
the *Cloth-trade*, either vnder the
Clothier, or vnder the *Merchant*.
Vnder the *Clothier*, either by *ill making*, or *falfe fealing* the Cloth.

For the making of good and true
Cloth, many excellent lawes haue
bin inuented & enacted by the wif-
dome of the *Parliaments* of this
land, from time to time. And the
Statute of 4. of the *King Cap*. 2.
doth feeme to bee an *Epitome* or
Compendiary of all the former Statutes in this kinde. In this Statute
is prefcribed, the true breadth, and
length, and waight, that may con-
duce to the making of a true and
perfect Cloth, Kerfie or Manufacture. If a Clothier make a Cloth
of leffe waight, then is fet downe
in

The decay of Clothing vnder the Clothier, or vnder the Merchant.

4. Iacob.

Vnder the Clothier, by ill making, or falfe fealing of Cloth.

in the said Statute, he offendeth in *Quantitie:* If of lesse breadth, or length, or of forbidden kindes of wooll, hee offendeth in *Qualitie.* If a Clothier offend in *neither* of these by his *owne act*, yet he may offend in *both*, by his *instruments* or *workemen* : Either by the *Weauers*, in *not putting in* the stuffe *at the making*; or by the *Tuckers* in *pulling out* the stuffe *after the making* thereof.

  A Cloth also may be well made, & yet false sealed. A Cloth may be said to be lawfully made, when it is truly sealed. For although it may be impossible to make some Clothes, iust of those quantities and qualities prescribed by the Statute; as the *Clothiers* terme is, *A man cannot cast a cloth in a mould:* yet I hope, they will giue me leaue to say, that it is possible that a Cloth may bee true sealed, though false made. And then a *Cloth ill made*, and *true*
sealed,

fealed, whereby the buyer may fee what he hath for his money, may bee faid to bee a good or lawfull Cloth according to the Statute.

Now the execution of the Statute for *Searching* and *Sealing of Clothes*, feemeth to be referred to two forts of men: which are either the *Aulnager* or *Searcher.* The *former* may feeme originally to haue beene an Officer appointed for that purpofe, as well by the *Notation* of the name, as by fome *Ancient Statutes.* For *Aulne,* and *Aulnage,* and *Aulnagier,* are all *French* words, taken from the meafuring of Cloth. And thence it is, that in that tongue they are wont to fay *Aulner draps* to meafure Clothes, by a *Trope* taken from the *Inftrument* by which they are *meafured.*

But becaufe the care of the *Aulnage* is committed to fo *Noble and Honourable a Perfonage,* that will not

11. *Hen.* 4. 6. &c.

not ſuffer any abuſe in the execution of that office : and the ſaid Statute of 4. *Iacobi* , and the former
Statutes of 39. and 43. *Elizabethæ*,
doe referre the *Searching* and *Sea-*
ling of Clothes, to certaine *Ouer-*
ſeers or *Searchers* , ſo called by the
ſaid *Statutes* , I will proceede vnto
them.

    And foraſmuch as *Execution* is
the *life* of the *law* , as H I s *Maie-*
ſtie in his *high wiſedome* admoni-
ſheth : and the *Prudence* and *Proui-*
dence of the *State*, haue beene very
great in deuiſing and enacting ſuch
good lawes from time to time, as
might tend to the encreaſe and aduancement of the *Drapery* of this
Kingdome : If therefore now any
thing bee amiſſe therein, it muſt
needs come through the want of
execution of thoſe *lawes. Hinc illæ*
lachrymæ ! This *Bonum* according
to H I s *Maieſties Regall rule*,is not
Benè . For theſe *Ouerſeers* and
                   Searchers

In His Maieſties ſpeech in Parliament. In Iune 1611.

Eâdem Oratione Regiâ.

Searchers beeing filly Countrey-
men, and generally not expert in
the *myftery* of making of Cloth:
in the *Search* whereof, there is as
much neede of skill as in the making: for how fhould they finde
the fault, that know not how it is
committed? Thefe Searchers I
fay, thus being ignorant and vnskilfull in their offices, and negligent alfo, (in which laft, 't hath
beene againe and againe confeft,
that they haue fet the feales of
their office, to Clothes they neuer
fearch't nor faw) needs muft there
be a great abufe, in the *execution* of
thofe good *lawes.*

   Nay I would I could not fay,
how much our Nation hath beene
vpbraided by the people of forreine parts with this abufe, that
the *Searchers Seales* of *England* are
bought and *fold* as in a market, and
put on the Clothes by the *Tuckers,*
and other the feruants of the
                         Clo-

Clothiers, as if the same had beene lawfully *Searched* and *Sealed* according to the *Statute*; when as the *Searchers Eye* neuer so much as beheld the *Clothes.*

Wherein the people of the *Netherlands* are so exact, that you shall neuer find any of their Countrey Clothes false *search't* or *sealed.* For you shall haue a *Seale* set vpon the Cloth when it commeth from the *Weauers:* another when it commeth frō the *Tuckers:* another whē it cōmeth from the *Dyers:* and that by men of good quality, appointed for that purpose in euery *City* and *Towne* where Cloth is made, termed *Curemasters:* so called from the *Care* they ought, and doe performe, in the execution of their office: wherein indeed they are so strict, that you shall neuer finde any of the *seales* aforesaid, set to any manner of *false* or *defectiue* Cloth.

For indeed the *Searcher* being a

sworne

sworne Officer,ought to be as a witnes without exceptió betwixt man
and man : that when a man feeth
the *Searchers feale* fet vpon the
Cloth,it fhould ferue as a true *Cer-
tificat* of the true making thereof.
It is a great impiety before *God*
and *Man*, to be a falfe witneffe in
any cafe : but thefe *Searchers* are
falfe witneffes *ipfo facto*,when they
doe *teftifie* to the world by their
feales, that thofe Clothes are *good
and true*, which indeede are vtterly *falfe*. And which aggrauateth
the matter yet more,that *the Kings
Seale of Armes*,which is *teftis omni
exceptione major*, fhould alfo be fet
to Clothes thus *falfely fearched* and
fealed; whereby not only *the Kings
fubiects*, but the *ftrangers* alfo in
forreine parts are deceiued, is a very groffe and grieuous abufe.

Amongft other abufes of this
kinde,one precedent come's to my
minde, of *ten* Clothes bought not
                                    long

An example
of Clothes
ill made,fear-
ched,and fea-
led.

long fince by a *Merchant*, of a *Clothier* of *Wiltfhiere*. Which Clothes were all *Sealed* by the *Searchers* of that place, for good & true, according to the Statute. But being tried by the *Merchant Buyer*, and afterwards by the *Sworne meafurer* of the Citie of *London*, were found fo defectiue in length, breadth and waight, that where thefe *ten* Clothes coft but 60. *lib.* or thereabouts, the faults in thefe *ten* Clothes came to neere 20. *lib.* which was one third part of the value of the Cloth. And it being a notable contempt of the law, the *Lords* of H i s *Maiefties moft Honourable Priuie Councell* were informed thereof; who were pleafed to fend down a *Meffenger* into that *County*, and fetch't vp both the *Clothier* and *Searchers*, who worthily vnder-went the Condigne Cenfure of the Lords.

Vnder the *Merchant* alfo the
E   Cloth

The Cloth-
trade fuffereth
vnder the
Merchant,
At home and
abroad.
At Home, by
Exportation
of the Mate-
rials, or Im-
pofition of
Charge.

Cloth-trade fuffereth both at *Home* and *Abroad*. *At Home,* by *Exporting the Materials,* either of *Woolles* or *Wooll-fels* from the *Sea-coafts* of *England,* and the *Kingdome* of *Ireland :* or by *Ouer-lading* the *Cloth-trade,* either with any *generall* or *fpeciall* charge.

The *latter* I cannot pretermit: for as the chiefe waight of the *Cloth-trade* lyeth on the *Merchants-Aduenturers ;* fo alfo is the burthen of charge moft felt vnder that *trade*. For the *Impofitions and Impreft money* by them laid vpon the *Cloth,* for defraying the charge of their Gouernment, and payment of their Debts ; hath driuen many good *Merchants* out of the trade, and giuen the *Clothiers* occafion to complaine of want of *Buyers,* and thruft the trade it felfe more and more into the *Strangers* hands.

Abroad by
vnfit Refi-
dence.

And *abroad,* by the *vnfit place of Refidence,* which the *Merchants-Aduenturers* are fallen vpon in

Holland. Whither they goe with
great perill of Shippe and Goods :
And where they come farre fhort
of that they hoped for; and of that
quicke and ample vent of their
Cloth they found in *Zeeland.* The
Agitation of which remooue ; is
vehemently fufpected to haue mo-
ued the *Merchants* of *Holland,* to
procure *Priuiledges* of the *States
Generall* to *Incorporate* themfelues,
and *keepe Courts,* to confront the
Merchants-Aduenturers ; which
they neuer did before : To haue
drawne the * *Taring* of Cloth into
Holland, where the *Buyers* are in
fome fort, *Iudges & Parties* ; which
before was in the *Mart-towne,*
where the *Seller* was prefent : And
laftly to haue haftned the great *Impofition* in *Holland.* All which are
matters of moment, and concerne
the *Cloth-trade* very much, and
whereof the *Englifh Factors* there
refiding doe generally complaine:

E 2 Yet

* That is, a-
bating for the
faults thereof.

Yet *Thefe* I rather inftance then vrge : leauing the further Ouerture thereof to their own relation.

Now the *forreine caufes* of the decáy of the *Drapery* of *England* : are either *generall*, as the warres in *Germany* : or *fpeciall* as the *great Impofition* lately laide vpon our Cloth in *Holland*.

Forreine caufes of the decay of the Draperie, are the warres,and the great Impofition in *Holland*.

By the *former*, the Courfe of Trade is ftopt and hindered , that Merchants cannot paffe without perill from place to place : and the monies become fo variable , that when a Merchant hath fold his Cloth, and hopeth to haue gained fomething thereby ; by that time that the terme for payment is expired, he receiueth leffe in value then the Clothes coft,by the *raifing* and *rifing* of the monies.

By the *latter*, the *Merchants* of the *Netherlands* are difcouraged, wherby many of them haue giuen ouer their trades , which heretofore they followed in ample man-

ner, vnto *Muſcouy* , the *Eaſt-Coun-
tries* and other places,in our *Engliſh
Clothes* bought of the *Merchants-
Aduenturers* from time to time.

Cap. III.
*Of gouerned Trade, and therein
of* Monopoly.

HItherto the *Matter of Trade*
hath beene conſidered in *Money* and *Merchandize* : the *Forme*
followeth , and that either in reſpect of *Gouernment*, or *want of Gouernment* in trade. *Gouernment* is a
repreſentation of the *Maieſtie* and
Authoritie of the KING. The ſubiect that is honoured with *Gouernment* , is inueſted with part of the
KINGS *Honour.* The *Trades* of this
Kingdome which *by* HIS *Maieſties
eſpeciall Grace and Fauour* are reduced vnder *Order and Gouernment*
into *Corporations, Companies* , and
Societies , doe certainly much
E 3 *Aduance*

Aduance and *Aduantage* the *Com-merce* of this *Common-wealth,* and farre excell the trades of any other forreine Merchants in their vngo-uerned trades.

But as the *Vſe* of *Gouernment* is excellent for the reſtraint of vnskil-full and diſorderly trade: ſo the *A-buſe* thereof is as inconuenient, if at any time the ſame be too ſtrict, and come within the compaſſe of a *Monopoly.* And becauſe the name and nature of *Monopoly,* is more *talk't of,* then well *vnderſtood* of many; and ſome thinke that the re-ducing of trade into *Order* and *Go-uernment,* is a kinde of *Monopoli-zing* and reſtraint of trade : I haue thought it not vnſeaſonable to be-ſtow ſome ſpeciall paines in the di-ligent inueſtigation thereof. Not that I would haue the trade of the *Kingdome,* ſo circumſcribed or ap-propriated to any, that others of H I s *Maieſties* ſubjects ſhould be depriued

depriued of the libertie thereof ;
but that vpon equall and reasona-
ble termes, trading vnder *Order* and
Gouernment , without that ill tin-
&ure of *Monopoly, the* Kings *high
way of trade* should be opened vnto
all.

The name therefore of *Monopoly* in our English tongue, is deriued,
as the learned know, of the Greeke
word Μονοπώλιον : whence also the La-
tine word *Monopolium* is borrow-
ed.   Some deriue it of Μόνος *Solus,*
and πωλέω *Vendo,* to sell alone.   O-
thers of Μόνος *Solus,* & πωλέουσι *Versor,*
to conuerse alone.   Others of Μόνος
Solus, and πόλις *Ciuitas , quasi vnica
negotiatio in Ciuitate.*   But all these
agree in one meaning of the word,
that it is *Singularis Negotiatio,* a di-
uerting of *Commerce* from the naturall course and vse thereof, into
the hands of some few, to their benefite, and others preiudice.   I also
find many *definitions* of *Monopolies:*
E 4   and

Huiufmodi contractus tanta emptionis & conductionis fimilitudine confundebatur, vt vix ac ne vix quidem à iuris confultis internofci poffit.
Hottom. ad tit. in lib. 18.& 19. De Rep. lib. 1. cap. 11.

and a great queſtion among the *Ciuilians*, whether a *Monopoly* may bee exerciſed of one alone ; and whether it conſiſt aſwell in *Locatio Conductio*, as they ſpeak, as in *Emptio Venditio*. Which laſt is out of queſtion with all. And of the former I finde an inſtance in *Ariſtotle* of *Thales Mileſius* his *Monopoly* : who by his knowledge in *Aſtrology*, foreſeeing one yeare in the winter, that there would be great plentie of oiles the next yeare, hired before hand all the places and engines for making of oile through both the Ilands of *Melazo & Chius*, and afterwards let out the ſame againe at his owne pleaſure & price. In the ſame place he maketh alſo mention of another, who bought vp all the Iron in *Sicilia*, which afterwards he ſold againe, and made one hundred talents of that which coſt him but fiftie. Amongſt others I will take the *definition* of
Althuſius

Politic.cap.31.
n.20.

Althusius for all the rest. *Monopoli-um,* saith he, *Est Commercium emen-di, vendendi, permutandiue, à paucis vel vno etiam vsurpatum, reliquis ciuibus præceptum, quo pretia augen-tur cum lucro negotiantis, & reliquo-rum damno.* That is, *Monopoly is a kinde of Commerce, in buying, selling, changing or bartering, vsurped by a few, and sometimes but by one per-son, and fore-stalled from all others, to the Gaine of the Monopolist, and to the Detriment of other men.*

The parts then of a *Monopoly* are twaine. The restraint of the liberty of *Commerce* to some one or few: and the setting of the price at the pleasure of the *Monopolian* to his priuate benefit, and the pre-iudice of the publique. Vpon which two hinges euery *Monopoly* turneth. And these two parts are respectiuely repugnant to the two fundamentall requisites of all good Lawes

Lawes: to wit, *Equity* and *Vtility.*
For it is againſt *Equity*, that one
member of a *Common-wealth*
ſhould be more free, then another
of equall ranke and condition. And
what can be more contrary to *Publique Vtility*, then that ſome one or
few perſons, ſhould ſway the price
of any thing vſefull to the *Common-wealth*, to their owne enriching, and the *common loſſe* of other
men? And here it is to bee well
obſerued, that vnleſſe theſe two
parts concurre in a *Monopoly*: it
cannot truely and properly be ſo
called, nor ought it ſo to bee ac-
counted. And therefore *Althuſius*
following *Decianus*, ſaith well of
that reſtraint of the *common liberty*,
which we call *Suit of Mill*: which
compelleth men to vſe this or that
Mill to grinde corne, and none o-
ther: that it doth onely *Sapere Monopolium*, Sauour of Monopoly:
but that it is not truely and properly

*Althuſius polit.
cap.32.
Tib.Decianus
tract.crim.
cap.21.
Menoch.lib.
2.n.569.*

ly a *Monopoly.* For in that cafe of *Suit of Mill*, vnleffe there be a greater tolle or recompence exacted for grinding, then at other Milles, it falleth onely within the firft part of a Monopoly, to wit, *of the reftraint of the publike liberty* ; but not within compaffe of the other part, *the fetting of the price.* But for this reftraint *of the publique liberty of Commerce,* it may be fo ordered by *the wifedome of the State,* that it may be both *Lawfull* and *Beneficiall* to the *Common-wealth.* Which affertion, becaufe it may feeme ftrange to fome, I will make euident by *good Authority* and *Examples.* Peter *Martyr* that famous light of the Churches of the Gofpell, defendeth the reftraint of *Solomon,* that none fhold buy *Horfes of Egypt* without his licence, to be Lawfull. And of this kinde is the *Preemption of Tinne* here in *England,* granted by H<small>I</small>s *Maiefties gracious*

P. Mart 1. *Reg. c.* 10. *&c.*

gracious letters Patents to fomefew,
with reftraint of all others: which
I dare boldly affirme is not onely
Lawfull,but very *Beneficiall* alfo to
this *Commonwealth*. For thereby
our *Thrice Noble Prince* receiueth a
good reuenue, and the *Tinne* of
this Land is fold for many thoufand pounds a yeare more in Forrein parts,then otherwife it would,
to the great increafe of the *Com-
monftocke* of this *Kingdome*. Alfo
the Law of this *Realme* alloweth,
that if any man inuent a new Art,
beneficiall to the *Common wealth*,
he may haue a Patent to vfe that
Arte folely, with reftraint of all
others for feuen yeares : as well in
recompence of his induftry, as for
the incouragement of others, to
ftudy and inuent things profitable
for the publique *Symbiofis*. The
Statutes of the *Kingdome* reftraine
from the exercife of fundry *Crafts*,
all fuch as haue not ferued an ap-
prentifhood

prentifhood vnto the art which they would exercife : to the ende that thofe artes might be brought to better perfection, and the things made, might be good and feruiceable for thofe that buy and vfe them.

The reftraint of the *Publique Liberty*, is fometimes exercifed by *Priuate Authority* : fometimes by *Publique*. Which diftinction is made by the *Emperour Zeno. Iubemus ne quis pro fua authoritate, vel facro elicito refcripto, &c. Monopolium audeat exercere.*

Cod.lib. 4. Tit. 59.

The *former*, is practifed when any one or more, haue by their owne priuate contracts, gotten any Commoditie or matter of *Commerce*, wholly into their owne hands. Of this kinde are the examples aboue cited out of *Ariftotle.*

The *latter*, is when by Publique Authority, the liberty of the fubiect

is

is reſtrained : which is done, ſometimes by the *Prerogatiue of the*
KING : ſometimes by *Act of Parliament.*

The *former*, by diſpenſing with
a generall Law in ſome point , and
applying the diſpenſation to ſome
one or fewe, with reſtraint of
others. The *latter*, by prohibiting
all, but ſome one or few perſons to
vſe the benefit of the Law in ſome
point or other.

For diſpenſing with the Lawes,
it is without queſtion, that *the*
KING hath power to diſpence
with a *Penall Law*, when it prohibi-
teth that which is not *Malum in ſe.*
For the *Parliament* hauing made
a *Statute* with intent of the *Publique good* : yet the ſame by reaſon
of ſomething not foreſeene at the
making of the Law, may proue ve
ry preiudiciall in the Execution.
And then the *Malum prohibitum*,
as the *Lawyers* ſpeake, may be diſ-
penced

penced with by *the* KING. Thus
the *Parliament* hauing prohibited
the exportation of white Clothes
vndreſt aboue the price of foure
pound the Cloth : the obſeruation of that Statute was found by
experience to be very preiudiciall
to the Trade, and free vent of the
Cloth in forreine parts.   Where-
upon Q. *Elizabeth,* granted a Speciall Licence to the Fellowſhip of
the *Merchant-Aduenturers,*to tranſ-
port all ſorts of white Clothes vn-
dre'ſt, with a *Non obſtante* to that
Statute. And although all other
men ſtood lyable to the Statute
ſtil,and were reſtrained, yet the *V-
tility* that hereby aroſe to the *Common-wealth,* did farre exceed the
reſtraint of the *Publique Liberty.*
For within few yeares after the
granting of this Licence , the vent
of Cloth in forreine parts increa-
ſed to twice as much, as formerly
it was during the ſtrict obſeruation
of

33.H.8.

of the Statute. Other like difpen-
fations of Statutes, I might inftance : as that of the 28. *H.8.* concerning the retailing of *Gafgoigne
Wines* at two pence a quart: which
is difpenced with, by a licence to
the *Company of the Vintners* : but
thefe may fuffice for euery mans
vnderftanding of this kinde of reftraint.

For *Prohibition by Act of Parliament* : fuch is the Act whereby all
the fubiects of this Realme, excep-
ting fuch as are of the Corporation of the *Mufcouy Company* , are
forbidden to trade into any part of
Ruffia. Alfo that of 3. *Iacob.* concerning *Artizan Skinnes*, whereby
all but that *Company*, are forbidden
to buy and retaile fome forts of
Skinnes. In thefe and the like, the
Parliament maketh reftraint of the
Common liberty of Commerce , and
the fame reftraint is againe relea-
fed, not vnto all, but to fome perfons

3. Iacob.

fons or *Corporations* by *fpeciall
exception and prouifo* of the Act of
Parliament.

*The latter kinde of reftraint by
Publique Authority,* is when that
which feemeth by the Lawe to be
free to all, is by fome *Patent or Proclamation of the Prince,* prohibited
to all, fauing fome certaine *Corporations,* or perfons fpecially excep-
ted and authorized in the fame *Patent* or *Proclamation.* Of this kind
are generally reputed all *Corporations* of *Merchants,* which are not
confirmed by *Act of Parliament.*
Which are generally reputed to
carry with them a reftraint to
others, of that *liberty,* which the
Law doth feeme to offer to all in
point of *Commerce.* Whence it is
that fo many pleade the *Freedome*
of fubiects, and *preffe,* or rather *oppreffe* that plea of equity, that it is
equall that all fubiects fhould bee
a like free to be Merchants in all
F   Trades.

Trades. To whom I anſwere, that firſt there is no good *Equality* in it, becauſe it is againſt the *Publique Vtility* that all ſhould bee Merchants at their pleaſure. For that's not equall, that may ſeeme profitable to one, and bee hurtfull to many. *Atque ipſa vtilitas iuſti propè mater & æqui,* as *Horace* ſpeaketh. And yet what point of equity is broken, when the freedome of Societies is ſo carried, that it is open to all men vpon equall termes; that is to ſay, either by ſeruice or purchaſe? Otherwiſe it were very vnequall, that one man ſhould ſerue for his freedome, or buy the ſame : and another man ſhould haue it for nothing. If this point were well thought vpon, I proſume the *Gracious Grants and priuiledges* of His *Maieſtie,* conferred vpon *Societies,* would not ſeeme ſo much a reſtraint of the *Common liberty,* as a prudent ordering

ring and accommodating thereof
vnto the *Publique Vtility*. For it
hath euer beene a *Policy* of this
State, to reduce the *Trades* of *Merchants* of this *Kingdome* into *Corporations* and *Societies*, for the aduancement of Trade, by the benefit of order and gouernment : well
foreseeing that there cannot be
any greater *Bane* to a *Well-gouerned
Common-wealth*, then *Ill-gouerned
and disorderly Trade*. Whereof I
shall haue fitter occasion to speake
in the next Chapter, when I come
to treat of the Inconueniences of
the want of gouernment in Trade.
So that in this case the generall rule
must be this; that such a restraint
of the *Publique Liberty*, as is before
mentioned, is alwayes to be allow-
ed, when the same is recompenced
with a *Publique Vtility*. According
to that of *Tacitus*, *Omne magnum   Tacitus.
exemplum habet in se aliquid iniqui,
quod vtilitate publicà contra singu-*

F 2   *los*

los compenſatur. Alſo the liberty that the Law ſeemeth to giue the ſubiects in Trade, is to be vnderſtood, of imployment *Within the Kingdome*, not *Without the Kingdome.* For what liberty can a *Nationall Law*, giue to a *Forrcin Trade* vnder a *Forreine Iuriſdiction*, when the liberty or reſtraint thereof dependeth vpon thoſe *Forreine Princes and States* where that Trade is tollerated? Therfore the *Law* may giue the ſubiect Liberty *Within the Land*, but it is *the* KING that muſt enable men to trade *Without the Land.* For all the *Trade* of the *Merchants* of this *Kingdome* into *Forreine Countries*, is grounded vpon the *Amity of the* KING, and the *Treaties of Peace* contracted by *the* KING, with the *Kings and Rulers* of thoſe *forreine parts*, at his owne charge, and by HIS owne Authoritie, without the aſſiſtance of HIS *Parliament.* And therefore it holdeth

deth good congruity , that *the* KING by HIS like Authority, may haue the difpofing and ordering of fuch HIS contracts at his owne pleafure.

The fecond part of *Monopoly* remaineth, of the *fetting of the price* at the pleafure of the *Monopolift,* to his *priuate gaine,* and the *publique loffe.* This *Gothofredus* calleth *the forme* of a *Monopoly.* And in truth it is the very *Soule* and *Accomplifh-ment* thereof. And he or they that haue this power ouer the price of the thing they negotiate,may well be faid according to the notation of *Monopoly* , from μόνος and πωλέω, to *conuerfe alone.* For in fo doing, they fo liue , as none can liue by them , in refpect of their finguler gaine in this kinde : Contrary to that honeft Prouerbiall rule of the Dutch , that men muft *Leuen ende laeten Leuen:*So Liue as other men may Liue by them. But here I

Cod.4. 59.

cannot but difcharge all thofe *Cor-porations* of this *Kingdome,* of this part of *Monopoly* , which afford to euery particuler trader thereof, the managing of his owne ftocke, in buying and felling as hee can, without any combination with others.   In which it is as impoffi-ble as vnufual, for any to haue com-mand of the price of their *Commo-dities* : becaufe there is fuch a mul-titude of Traders of them; and euery man is at liberty to buy or fell, without any rule by any gene-rall order , or meanes to hold one price. But the greateft fufpition of *Monopoly* in *Corporations* , is in fuch as Trade, in *Ioint ftockes.* Whereof if there be any that tra-deth in a *Ioint ftocke* , and hath the *Sole* buying or felling of any *Com-modity* , and buy and fell the fame *Iointly,* as by one perfon or com-mon factor, fuch is guilty of *Mono-poly.*

For *particuler men*,they may alfo commit *Monopolizing*: either
by procuring *Patents* by mifinfor-
mation of the *State*,for the *Sole Im-
porting* or *Exporting*,buying or felling at their owne prifes, to the
reftraint of the *Common Liberty*,
and the *Publique Vtility* of the
Kingdome : or elfe when fome one
or few, without any Authority,
doe ioine together to engroffe and
buy in a Commodity, and fell it
out againe at their owne price. Of
the former kinde, are thofe *Cata-
logue* of crying *Monopolies* , which
HIS *Maieftie* in HIS *high Wifedome and Grace* damned in HIS
Princely Proclamation of the tenth
of *Iuly* laft,in the xix.yeare of HIS
*Maiefties moft happy Reigne ouer
this Kingdome* : Many of which
were abufed in the *Practife*, from
that which they appeared to be in
the *Inftitution.* And here a pret-
ty queftion occurreth. When a
F 4 *Patent*

Patent is granted to a certaine per-
son or persons, so as hee or they
haue power to licence others to
exercise some kinde of *Commerce*
solely, and consequently with
command of the price : the question is, who is then the *Monopolian,*
whether the *Patentees*, or their
Assignes? In this case I suppose,
that both the one and the other
commit *Monopoly*. For first, the
Patentees make their price at their
pleasure vpon their *Assignes*, and
they againe vpon the *subiects*. So
that here is *Monopoly* vpon *Mono-*
poly : like your *Salt* vpon *Salt, Inte-*
rest vpon *Interest*, or the *Decompo-*
situm in *Grammer.*

In the latter, some sorts of
Tradef-men in *London*, are said to
offend. Which being matters of
Generall note, and willing to auoid
offence, I will passe by such parti-
culars. And this shall suffice for
the *Definition* and *Distribution* of
Monopoly.   CAP.

CAP. IIII.

Of want of Gouernment in Trade.

SVch is the *Forme of Trade* cõſidered in the *Strict Vſe* or *Abuſe* of *Gouernment*, by way of *Monopoly*. It now remaineth briefely to ſhew the *Too Looſe Vſe* thereof, by *Vngouerned Trade*.

It is a *Maxime* in the *Mathematiques*, that *Rectum eſt Index ſui & obliqui*. And the want of *Gouernment*, cannot better be demonſtrated, then by the benefit of *Gouernment* it ſelfe. For thereby the *Common-wealth* hath beene much aduantaged, both in the encreaſe of the natiue Commodities of the *Kingdome*, and the aduancement of their vſe and price in *Forreine parts*: and alſo in keeping the forreine

reine wares at a moderate rate
within this *Kingdome.* This will
be yet more perfpicuous, if we caft
our eye firft vpon the feueral *Societies of Merchants* which trade *vnder Gouernment:* and then on thofe
which trade *without Gouernment.*
For *Contraria juxta fe pofita, magis
elucefcunt.*

In the firft place therefore confider we that *Ancient* and heretofore
famous fellowfhip of the *Merchants-
Aduenturers of England.* Hath
it not by their politique rule and
order, eaten out the *Societie* of the
Hans-townes of *Germanie* and the
Merchants of the *Entercourfe* of the
Low Countries, in thofe trades,
which a long time they enioyed in
this land? And whereas thofe of
the *Hans*, vented in *Germany*, only a
matter of *fixe thoufand* of our
Clothes yeerely and at low prifes :
and held this *Realme* as it were be-
holding vnto them for their fhip-
ping

The Mer-
chants-Ad-
uenturers.

ping: yea vpon fome difcontent
for denying of them priuiledges,
durft offer fome hoftilitie in the
time of *Edward* the fourth. Wher-
as the *Merchants-Aduenturers* by
their *Charters*, granted from time
to time by the *Princes of this
Realme*, and fauoured by *Parliaments* fucceffiuely; by their orderly mannaging of their trade, haue
fupplanted the trade of the *Hanfes*
in *Germany* : and brought the faid
Sixe thoufand vented by them in
Germany, vnto *Thirtie thoufand*
Clothes yeerely & at great prifes.
And it is worthy to be remembred
to their *Honour*, that feruice which
the *Merchants-Aduenturers* did to
the *State* in *Anno.* 88. when they
fupplied the *Nauie Royall* with a
whole fhips lading of *Powder and
Shot* from *Hamburgh*: which came
luckily euen *in articulo temporis*,
when there was a very great want
thereof. Thefe alfo haue from
time

time to time employed and bred vp many worthy Mafters of fhips and Mariners: and built many Tall, warlike and Seruiceable fhippes: which as they themfelues alfo, are at all times ready to doe feruice to the KING & STATE vpon all occafions. None of all which they had euer beene able to haue done as particular men, in a loofe, diftracted, and diforderly trade.

Great benefit alfo hath arifen from the *Eaft-land Company*: who haue wonne like ground of the *Hanfes* of the *Baltique Sea*: and doe employ in that trade a great number of proper *Shippes* and *Men*.

The *Leuant Company* likewife by their trade vnder *Gouernment*, hath built a great ftrength of warlike, Tall & Lufty Shipping, which they employ in that trade: and by their induftry haue wonne from the *Italians* the trade of the *Leuant*: the *Commodities* whereof were before brought

The Eaftland Companie.

The Leuant Company.

brought into this *Realme* by *Argo-sies* to the encreafe of *forreine fhip-ping*, and at *deare* rates: and is now reduced to the *Natiues* of this *Kingdome*, to the encreafe of *Ship-ping*, and the benefit of the *Pub-like*. Which without *Gouernment* and good order, had been impoffible for them to haue done.

The *French Company* alfo, though but lately reduced to *Order*, haue reformed many abufes in that trade, in maintaining the *Natiue Commodities* of this *Kingdome* in much better eftimation, and in kee-ping the *Forreine* at moderate pri-ces: and in employing greater fhipping, then at any time before. Which were impoffible for them to effect *Singly*, without *Societie*.

The French Company.

Laftly, for the *Eaft-India Com-pany*, whereof I am preuented to fay what I might, by two feuerall difcourfes publifhed in print, the one by that worthy and rarely qua-lified

The Eaft-India Com-pany.

lified Gentleman Sr *Dudley Digges* Knight, the other by that difcreete *Merchant* M. *Thomas Mun*: yet this I fay, that this *Great and Noble Societie* by the benefite of *Gouernment*, hath fet on foot a very *mightie Trade*, farre beyond any other *Company* of this *Kingdome*: and accordingly hath excelled in greatneffe of fhipping, and making Mariners of land-men, beyond the example of any other Corporation: & had not *Enuie* thought that *Trade* too great a *Treafure* for this *Kingdome*, doubtleffe they had in *Encreafe of trade*, excelled all the *Companies* of *Merchants* in this *Common-wealth.*

But here the ordinary obiection encountereth me, that in *Germany, Spaine, France, Italie,* and the *Netherlands,* there are no fuch *Companies*, nor *reftraint of Merchants*, as here in *England*: and yet that thofe *Countries* thriue better in their trades.

The obiection anfwered, that the Merchants of other countries trade without gouernment, which is examined by a particular enumeration of diuers Countries.

Trades, then we in ours. I anfwer, that if it be granted, that they haue no fuch *Companies* nor *reftraints* of any, and that they thriue better in their trades then we; yet it will not follow, that this their better thri-uing is becaufe euery man is at li-bertie to be a *Merchant* at his plea-fure. This is the *fallacy* which the *Logicians* call Τὸ μὴ αἴτιον ὡς αἴτιον; *Non caufa pro caufa.* For if that were the caufe, why then fhould not our *Spanifh Trade*, that hath no *Compa-ny* nor *reftraint*, profper better the the other Trades which are *Gouer-ned in Companies?* whereas to fpeak as the truth is, *This* Trade & *Thefe Merchants*, are the moft miferable of all the other *Trades* and *Trades-men* of this *Kingdome*, and all through want of *Gouernment*: tho-rough whofe fides the *Common-wealth* fuffereth, and hath already loft many Millions in value of the *wealth* of the *Weale-publique*, as I
fhall

shall shew anone. But to the *Af-sumption*.I deny that the *Merchants* of those *forreine Countries*, trade without *Gouernment*. For *Germany* hath anciently had one *Society*, or *Corporation* of *Merchants* in all their *Sea-townes*, called the *Societie* of the *Hans* before noted : as their houses of *Staple* yet standing at *Bridges* in *Flanders*, *Antwerpe* in *Brabant*, *Nouogrode* in *Rufsia*, *Bergen* in *Norwaye*,and the *Steelyard* in *London* can witnes. Which Trade of theirs flourished , as long as it continued vnder *Gouernment* : but hauing lost their *Priuiledges*, partly by their owne *Stragling*,and partly being ouertop't by the flourishing of the *Merchants-Aduenturers Trade*, their Trade is now almost quite fallen to the ground.

For *Spaine* and *Portugall*: all men know that their *Sea Trade* is little, sauing to the *East* and *West Indies*. And those Trades are carried which

As first Germany.

Spaine and Portugall.

with *Gouernement* , and farre more reſtraint then ours.

For *France,* there are not (that I know) any *Companies* of *Merchants* for forreine parts. Which I take to be the cauſe , why thoſe Merchants ſhipping, is of ſo ſmall burthen, and of as little ſufficiency for ſeruice. Which is an effect of a ſtragling vngouerned Trade.

For *Italy,* that conſiſteth of ſo many ſeuerall *Iuriſdictions,* that it were impoſſible to make a generall *Corporation* for any one kinde of *Sea-Trade.* For example, were it not in vaine for *Genoa* to make a *Corporation* & *Orders* for Trade, whileſt *Florence* held a contrary courſe? It were certainly all one, as to haue a *Company* of Merchants for *Spaine* at *London* , and the *Weſt-parts* left looſe to Trade without *Order* or *Gouernment* , which were a meere mockery. But the Trade in many parts of *Italy* , being carried by

G *Families,*

Families, and euery *Family* being as it were one Perſon, there is a kind of *Gouernment* in their Trades, and the ſame performed with merueilous credite, policie, and iudgement.

The *Lowe Countries*, by that *Vnion* which is of the ſeuerall *Townes and Prouinces* vnto the *States Generall* (which neuertheleſſe is as much, and endureth as long, as euery ſeuerall *Prouince and Towne* liſteth,) haue of late yeares erected their *Eaſt India Company*, and the like for *Guiny*, and are in hand with the like for the *Weſt Indies*. Alſo the *Cloth-buyers*, the principall *Merchants of Holland*, haue lately obtained *Octroy* ſo termed, which is *Priuiledges and Immunities* of the *States*, to aſſemble themſelues, and to keepe Courts, and make Orders for their Trade ; and principally to confront & oppoſe the *Merchants-Aduenturers* Trade, vpon ſome diffe-

differences, lately fallen out betwixt thofe *Cloth-buyers* and the
faid *Company* about the *refidence*
before noted.   For their other
Trades of *Germany, Poland, England, France* and *Spaine*, they rather wifh then finde it poffible, to
ioine the feuerall *Townes* in one
Rule and Order. And who fo çon-
uerfeth with that *Nation,* fhal finde
that they very much complaine of
the diforders of their Trades, for
want of that kinde of *Gouernment,*
which many of them take notice
of here in *England* : and fome of
them of late haue defired inftructi-
ons from hence in that behalfe.
Befides all this, thefe people as
they are borne and bred in an *Vni-
ted Country*, fo doth their nature
and difpofition encline much to an
Vnion and *Communion* in Trade.
Infomuch as oftentimes they are
able to worke their feates by *Con-
federacy* and *Combination*, againft

an *Incorporation* in our *Nation*. For they wisely consider, that their interest is inuolued in the *Publique* : where, in our *Nation*, men commonly preferre their *Particuler*, to the *Common good*.

And thus hauing answered the obiections against *Corporations,* of *Merchants* and *Gouerned Trades,* and shewed the many and manifold benefits arising to the *Common-wealth* thereby : It is now easie to shew the Iniury and Inconuenience to this *Common-wealth* by the want of *Gouernment in Trade*. Those that Trade without *Order* and *Gouernment,* are like vnto men, that make *Holes* in the bottome of that *Ship*, wherein themselues are *Passengers*. For want of *Gouernment* in Trade, openeth a gap and letteth in all sorts of vnskilfull and disorderly persons : and these not only sinke themselues and others with them ; but also marre
                                    the

the Merchandize of the land, both
in eſtimation and goodneſſe : then
which there can bee nothing in
Trade more preiudiciall to the
Publique Vtility. And to make
good theſe particulers, I take this
for a ground: *Nemo naſcitur artifex.*
Which as it is true in the occupati-
ons of *Artizans* : ſo is it much
more true in the *Trades* of *Merchants* : wherein there is ſo great
variety of difficult points to bee
learned, before a man can learne
his *Stucke,* as the Dutch-men ſpeak,
or be his *Crafts maſter.* And how
can the *Merchant* , that hath no
skill in his Commodity , looke to
it , that the Maker performe his
part? Or how can a falſified Commodity , hold his eſtimation and
vſe? The ill experience whereof,
is not more remarqueable in any
of HIS *Maieſties* ſubiects, then in
thoſe that trade into the *Dominions* of the *King* of *Spaine,* without

G 3   *Order*

Order or *Gouernment* in Trade. For
at the beginning of H I s *Maiesties*
moſt happy Raigne ouer this
Kingdome, this Trade by H I s *Maieſties Princely fauour*, was made a
Corporation and *Society* of *Merchants*, and flouriſhed vnder *Gouernment*. And then the new *Draperies*, and other the *Natiue Commodities* of the *Kingdome* were
maintained in their eſtimation and
goodneſſe at *Home and Abroad*:
But ſoone after by the clamour of
ſome who preferred their owne liberty, to the vtility of the publique, and by ſome misinformation
giuen the *Parliament* of that time,
this *Company* after it had flouriſhed
two yeares, was diſſolued, and euer
ſince expoſed to confuſion and diſ-
order in Trade, and is become a re-
ceptacle and *Rendes-vous* for euery
Shopkeeper, Stragler, and Vnskilful
perſon : and may ſerue for a liuely
repreſentation of the hopes that
may

may be expected, by such a loose
trade, as many now a daies so much
desire, not rightly conceiuing or
considering the benefit of *Gouernment,* nor the Inconueniencies that
doe perpetually accompany trade
in the want thereof. Which in the
Effects will be more *perspicuous,* to
which in their Order we now proceede.

Cap. V.

Of the Effects of the former Causes as they concerne the King.

SVch were the *Causes* considered in the *Matter* and *Forme* of
trade. The *Effects* follow: which
doe either concerne the King or
the *Common-wealth.*
 Such as are the *Causes,* such also
must needs be the *Effects* arising
G 4 from

from the fame : and thofe doe either refpect *the* K I N G in point
of *Honour,* or in point *of Renenue :*
and both in the *Matter* and *Forme*
of Trade.

Effects to the
King in point
of Honour.

    In point of *Honour,* there is a re-
·lation to the K I N G from the *Matter* of Trade, confidered *Generally,*
or *Specially.*

    Generally, in the generall neglect
of all trades, by temerous, rafh, and
litigious fuites of law : whereby
the *Peace* of the *Kingdome* is diftur-
bed, the *Iuftice* thereof abufed, and
in both the K I N G difhonoured.

    Or *Specially* in fome fpeciall
Commerce of this *Kingdome,* abufed
by *the* K I N G s Subiects, or Strangers. By *the* K I N G s Subiects, in
the *Drapery* of the *Kingdome,* when
H I s *Maiefties· Seale of Armes,*
which, as I faid, is, *Teftis omni exceptione maior,* fhall be difhonoured
by falfe Cloth and other Manu-
factures·, that are vnworthily
honoure d

honoured therewith : and whereby, those that buy the same both
within and *without* the Land , are
perswaded the same is good and
true,when the same is vtterly false:
which is a great indignity offered
to the KING.

By *Strangers* , in the *East India*
Action,and the matter of *Fishing*.
In the *East India Action* certainely the KINGS *Honour* is interessed;
not onely to protect his subiects
against the Iniuries done them by
the *Dutch* in the *East Indies* ; but
also to maintaine the *Glory and*
Renowne , *of* HIS *Sacred Fame*,
which hath heretofore beene *Illu-*
strious euen vnto the *Heathen* :
which some haue dared to doe
what they could to obscure. The
Fishing hath also reference to *the*
KINGS *Honour* : for it is a *Royalty*
of the *Crowne*, which the KING in
Honour cannot but protect.

　　There is also an *Effect* that ex-
tendeth

tendeth it felfe to *the* Kings *Honour* in the *Forme* of Trade, as it is *too ftrict,* or *too loofe. Too ftrict,* in refpect of *Monopolies*, wherein the *Prerogatiue of the* King is abufed, and therein His *Honour* alfo, by thofe that thereby feeke to priuiledge and Patronize things vnlawfull.

Too loofe, in the diforderly Trade of the fubiects out of *Gouernment.* For thofe *Strangers* that haue not beene in our *Countrey,* nor feene the Order of His *Maiesties Gouernment,* muft needes *Ex Vngue Leonem,* gueffe at the *Soueraigne* by the *Subiect* : And like to *Archimedes* who drew the whole pourtraiture of *Hercules* body, by his footftep onely found in Mount *Olympus,* proportion the *Royall and Regall Gouernment of* His *Maieftie at home ,* by the deportment of his fubiects *abroad.* And as the Orderly Trade of *Merchants*

chants is an *Honour to the* King, when the same is contained within the listes of *Gouernment*; so the contrary cannot choose but produce a quite contrary effect.

In point of *Reuenue* the Kings treasure is diminished, in the *Matter* also and *Forme* of Trade.   In the *Matter* of Trade, either in the *General* course of Trade, or in some *Particulers*. Inthe *Generall*, the great want of money, and decay of Trade throughout all callings and conditions of men, must needes cause a great diminution of His *Maiesties Reuenue*, both in His *Customes* and *Supplies*. For the *Customes*, those perpetually rise and fall with Trade : And for *Supplies*, the subiects being impouerished through want of Money and decay of Trade, are disabled to doe that seruice to His *Maiestie*, which otherwise they would be willing, and heretofore haue beene able to performe,

In point of Reuenue.

performe, in flourishing times of Trade. And if our experience hereof had beene in the θεωρια and not in the πραξις, in the *Contemplation* only, and not in *Action*: we had been much more happy in this *Kingdom* and *Nation*.

In the *particuler* courfe of Trade, it fhall content me to inftance onely the *Eaſt India Action*, and the *Fiſhing*, before referred to the Kings *Honour*, here to His *Reuenue*. By the *Eaſt India Action* there is a very great loffe to *the* King in His *Cuſtomes*, by the loffe of all the *Cuſtome* which that Trade would haue produced in all this time : and of the *Encreaſe* alſo of *Trade*, which that employment had brought with it, which would haue yeelded to His *Maieſty* a great *Increaſe* of *Cuſtomes* anſwerable to the ſame. Of both which if we had not beene depriued, certainely His *Maieſties Ferme of* His

Cuſtomes

Cuſtomes had yeelded *Many Thou-ſand pounds a yeare*, more then now they haue done.

By the *Fiſhing*, the *Cuſtomes and Tolles* which are vndoubtedly due to H I s *Maieſty* for the Strangers *Fiſhing* vpon our *Coaſts*, together with the encreaſe of Trade, and conſequently of *Cuſtomes* thereby alſo, wold amount to ſo great a va-lue, that I cannot wonder enough, that the ſame hath beene neglected all this while.

And laſtly in the *Forme* of Trade, *the* K I N G s *Reuenue* is migh-tily diminiſhed, when by the diſ-order of Trade, the very courſe of Trade is inuerted, and therein the K I N G s *Cuſtomes* and *Subſidies* alſo.

C A P.

Cap. VI.

Of the Effects of the former Causes
as they concerne the Com-
mon-wealth.

FRom *the* King, come to the *Kingdome.* Wherein there are also manifold *Effects* of the precedent *Causes,* both in the *Matter* and *Forme* of *Trade:*

And although in the very same things, wherein the *Honour* and *Reuenue* of *the* King are inuested, the *Wealth* of the *Common-wealth* is also interessed; yet the same may otherwise be distinguished, that so they may be made the more perspicuous and cleere to euery mans iudgement.

Effects to the Common-wealth Actiue and Passiue.

The *Effects* then that arise out of the *Matter* of *Trade* and fall vpon the *Kingdome,* may be saide to
be

be either *Actiue* or *Passiue*. *Actiue*, when they are done by *our Selues* : *Passiue*, when they are done to vs by *others*. *Actiue*, in the vse of *Law*, either *Too much*, or *Too little*. *Too much*, in *Suits of Law*, whereby one subiect vexeth another: which make this peaceable Kingdome seeme to bee at Warre within it selfe. For whilest men are thus at *Deadly feude* in Law, by the losse of their Times, and Trades, and States, the thrift of the *Commonwealth* must needes be neglected. *Too little*, In the *Non-execution* of *Lawes*, which tend either to the enlargement of *Clothing*, or the restraint of the Excesse of the *Kingdome*. The *former* is, either in respect of the *Ill searching* and *Sealing* of Cloth, or in the *Transportation* of the *Materials* of our Cloth before mentioned. In the *former* of these, the *Merchants Aduenturers* can giue you an account of *Ten thousand*

thousand pounds a yeare at least losse to this *Common-wealth*, by the *Tare* or abatements vpon the Cloth in forreine parts, for the false making and sealing thereof: Besides the other *Effects* of the decay of the *Drapery* it selfe, and other Trades depending thereon, the losse whereof is vnvaluable. In the *latter*, euery man is sensible of the losse to the *Common-wealth*, in robbing it of the *Materials*: whereby not onely our *Draperies* are *Impaired*, but the *Forreine* also are thereby much *Improued*.

Also the want of restraint of the *Excesse* of the *Kingdome*, in *Vsury* and *Prodigality*: the one being a *Viper* in a *Kingdome* that gnaweth through the bowels thereof: the other a *Canker* that fretteth and wasteth the stocke, in spending the forreine wares, more then it venteth of our owne: both and either doe

doe produce intollerable effects in a wel ordered *Kingdome* and Common-wealth.

Or *Paſſiue,* in the ill *Effects* that fall vpon the *Kingdome,* in things done to vs by *others.* And that either by *Friends* or *Foes. The for-mer* is done by *Impoſition,* or *Vſurpation.* By *Impoſition,* in the *Merchants Aduenturers* Trade in *Holland:* where there is lately taxed vpon a Pack Cloth 9. *Gilders;* vpon a long Cloth 18. *Gilders,* and vpon a fine Cloth 24. *Gilders,* which is 18. 36. and 48. ſhillings of our money. And yet neuertheleſſe they free their owne Countrey Cloth of all manner of charge ; nay, they giue encouragement to the makers thereof by many *Priuiledges and Immunities:* whereby it is more then manifeſt that they do what in them lyeth, to *Plant* their owne *Draperies,* and to *ſupplant*

H   ours

ours, to the infinite disaduantage of this *Kingdome.*

By *Vsurpation,* those Friends of ours, depriue vs of our *East India Trade,* and *Fishing,* which here againe occurre, and offer themselues for this purpose also. By *the former,* the *Common-wealth* hath not onely been dispossest all this while of so great a Stocke, as is that of the *East India Company,* but of the employment and encrease of Trade also, that thereby in all this time would haue accrewed vnto this *Kingdome.* And it is to be feared, that their policy is not onely to depriue the *Company* of their *Stocke,* but the *Kingdome* also of the *Trade* : which they thinke too great and glorious a *Fortune* for this *Common-wealth* to enioy, and the onely hope of their's. And hence it is that the *Restitution* is so hard to be had, because they think by detaining it, and spinning out

the

the time, they shall in time *weary*
and *weare* vs out of that Trade:
And so in the meane while, by
Plowing vp those *Indian Seas and
Soyle* with our *Heifers*, they may
at last *Reape* all the *Haruest*, and
possesse and dispossesse at their
owne pleasure, to the wonderfull
enriching of their *Common-wealth,*
and the impouerishing of *our s.*

By *the latter*, to wit, their *Fishing vpon our Coasts*, the *Common-
wealth* looseth that which they
gaine: which is merueilous in-
crease of *Trade*, of *Shippes*, and
Marriners. Whereby their *Nauigation* is mightily *Strengthened,*
their *Marriners multiplyed*, and
their *Trade* encreased: Of all
which this *Common-wealth* is depriued, and *their's* enriched.

By *Foes* also this *Common-
wealth* is lamentably *Paßiue*, in the
cruelty done by Turkish Pirats vpon *Men* and *Shippes*, and *Goods.*

H 2   The

The griefe is lamentable, the losse intollerable.

Lastly, there are ill Effects that fal vpon the *Common-wealth* in the *Forme of Trade* : and that in respect of *Monopolies*, or *Vngouerned Trade.* By *the former,* this *Common-wealth* is depriued of that true liberty of Trade, which belongeth to all the subiects: when the Commodity of some few, is preferred to the publique good.

By *the latter,* which is most remarqueable in the Trade of H I s *Maiesties* subiects into the Dominions of the *King* of *Spaine*, and the *Mediterrean* Sea; the Trade of this *Kingdome* consisting in *Bayes, Perpetuanoes, Kersies, Waxe, Tinne, Lead,* and other the *Natiue Commodities* of this *Kingdome,* is betrayed into the hands, both of those with whom we are in *Amitie,* and others that are with vs in *Enmity.* The one taketh aduantage of our vn-merchant-

merchant-like courſes for lacke of
Order : The other, of our Shippes
ſent foorth ſtragling for lacke of
Fleets : and both through want of
Gouernment in Trade. Whereby
the *Perpetuanoes* and other *new
Draperies* haue by little and little
bin made worſe and worſe, ſo that
now they are become quite out
of vſe, the *Trade loſt*, the *Traders
ruinated*, the *Manufactures by other
Nations ſupplied*, the *Nauigation
hindered*, by the loſſe of many *worthy men*, and *Seruiceable Shippes* :
In all which, the *Decay of Trade*
is exceeding *Great*, the *Common-
wealth's* loſſe *Infinite*.

H 3　　　Cₐₚ.

CAP. VII.

*Of the Remedy for all the former
Caufes of decay of
Trade.*

HAuing fhewed the many and
manifold *Caufes* of the decay
of Trade in the *Matter* and *Forme*
thereof : It remaineth now to prefent the *Remedy.* Which according to the precedent Method, I
will apply vnto all the particulers
in their order. Onely the *Remedies* for the *Effects,* I fhall prefent
in the *Caufes* : for the *Caufes* being
remoued, the *Effects* muft needs
ceafe , according to the common
Maxime in *Philofophy, Sublatâ cau-
fâ tollitur effectus.*

In my former diftribution I confidered the *Caufes* of the decay of
Trade, in the *Matter* and *Forme*
thereof :

thereof: and in the *Matter* I infi-
fted on *Money and Merchandize.*
The *Caufes* of the want of money,
I fhewed fome to be *Immediat*;
fome *Mediat* or remote. The *Immediat* Caufes, I noted to be fuch,
as either hinder the *Importation*;
or fuch as caufe the *Exportation*;
and both in the *Vnder-valuation* of
HIS *Maiefties* Coine. The *Remedy* offer's it felfe, which is double.
Firft, how it may be got : and next
how it may be kept. *The former*
may be done two wayes : By Raifing of the KINGS Coine ; and by
making current *Forreine Coines* at
equall value. *The latter,* alfo may
be done two wayes : By another
manner of Execution of the Statute for Employments then heretofore : wherein there is fome rea-
fon not to expreffe my felfe as I
might : And by HIS *Maiefties
Princely and Prudent Negotiation,*
with the *Princes* of our *Neighbour*

The Remedy
of drawing
money into
the King-
dome, muft
needs be the
raifing therof.

And by ma-
king forreine
Coines cur-
rant at like
value.

bour Countries, the *States* of the v-
nited *Prouinces* especially, to keepe
a more constant course in the values of their Coines. Neither of
which can be done by that *Par* of
Exchange, which is now againe in
agitation, and hath taken more then
twenty yeeres to bring it to perfection. Wherein, *absit inuidia ver-
bo*, that I say, there is neither *Pa-
rity*, nor *Purity.* For it is not the
rate of Exchanges, but the value of
monies, here lowe, elsewhere high,
which cause their Exportation:
nor doe the Exchanges, but the
plenty or scarcity of monies cause
their values. Or if I should grant
that to be the cause which is not :
yet it doth not follow, that because
the Stranger, like enough, would
be a deliuerer heere of money at a
high rate, that therefore the English must take it. And then the
consequence will be ill : for if the
rate be such as the *Taker* like not,
then

then the *Deliuerer* is yet more
thruſt vpon the exportation. But
this I leaue to thoſe to whom this
proiect is committed, with this,
that this opinion ſeemes to be *ciuſ-*
dem farinæ, with another of his, in
his *Canker of Englands Common-*
wealth, in theſe words: *And it were*
to be wiſhed, that our Cloth were ſold
at ſo deare a rate, and according to
the price of forreine Commodities,
that thereby other nations would
take vpon them to make our Clothes
themſelues : which might eaſily bee
remedied, by ſelling our woolles the
dearer, whereof they muſt make them.
Which ſeemes to haue in it much
more *Dutch* then *Engliſh*, to depriue this *Kingdome* of ſo Royall a
Manufacture, whereby ſo many
thouſands of poore families, are
maintained in the ſame : as if hee
would cure one Canker with another, contrary to our *Sauiours Ar-*
gument, that Satan cannot caſt out
Satan.

Satan. But I returne to mine owne *Station* : and therein to anſwer the obiections that doe occurre the raiſing of *Money* : which are wont to be principally, either the continuall *Raiſing* of it,to follow the *Riſing* of forreine Coine ; or elſe the ineuitable loſſe that thereby will fall, *Generally* vpon all men in the endearing of all things ; and *Particulerly* vpon *Landlords* and *Creditors*, in their rents and contracts.

For the continuall *Raiſing* of the Coine, that will be needleſſe, if the meanes be ſufficient for executing the *Statute* for *employments*, whereby the *Money* may be kept within the land when we haue it. And for the deareneſſe of things, which the *Raiſing* of *Money* bringeth with it, that will be abundantly recompenſed vnto all in the plenty of *Money*, and quickning of Trade in euery mans hand. And that which is equall to all, when hee that buye's

deare

deare ſhall ſell deare, cannot bee ſaid to be iniurious vnto any. And it is much better for the *Kingdome*, to haue things deare with plenty of *Money*, whereby men may liue in their ſeuerall callings : then to haue things cheape with want of *Money*, which now makes euery man complaine.

Laſtly, for *Landlords and Creditors*, their loſſe is eaſie to be preuented by *Prouiſo*, that the *Contracts* made before the raiſing of the *Monies* ſhall be paide at the value the *Money* went at, when the *Contracts* were made: according to the diſpoſition of the *Ciuill Law* in this caſe : *Valor monetæ conſiderandus & inſpiciendus eſt à tempore contractus, non autem à tempore ſolutionis.*

Gailius 2. *lib. Obſeruat. cap.* 73.

The raiſing alſo of the *Coine*, would raiſe the price of *Plate* : whereby either there would bee leſſe ſuperfluity that way, or elſe
more

more old *Plate*, which perhaps in fome mens hands is kept vp for *Treafure*, would be brought out, to be molten into *Coine*.

The *Mediate* or Remote *Caufes* of the want of *Money*, I obferued to bee either *Domeftique or Forreine*. The *Domeftique*, *Generall or Speciall*. The *Generall*, the great *Exceffe* of the *Kingdome*, in confuming the Commodities of forreine Countries in fuch abundance, to our owne loffe. And amongft thofe, the great exceffe in *Tobacco* is none of the leaft: which if it might feeme good to the High Wifedome of His *Maieftie*, to reftraine, or at leaft to giue a tolleration of the *Virginia* and *Barmudo's* only : there might be a great deale of *Pietie* and *Policy* fhewed in this *Remedy*. For in the one refpect, it would tend to a great enriching of that plantation, which fo happily fucceedeth through Gods bleffing: and

A Remedy for exceffe.

and in the other it would aduantage the KING and the *Kingdome*,
in the redreſſe of the diſorder of
the *Spaniſh Trade*, and in bringing
in *Treaſure* in ſtead of that *Toye*,
more then the Rent that is now rai-
ſed to HIS *Maieſtie* for the ſame.

The Superfluity of other Commodities may bee reſtrained by
lawes *Veſtiary* and *Sumptuary*, according to the example of *Germany*
& other our Neighbor Countries.

The *Speciall Remote Cauſe* of our
want of *Money*, I noted to bee the
want of our *Eaſt India Stocke* in the
Common-wealth. The *Remedy* wher-
of, is in the *Princely Power and Gra-
tious Fauour* of HI s *Maieſtie* to
apply at HIS pleaſure to this
Languiſhing body. And if HI s
Sacred Maieſtie will vouchſafe to
apply HIS Gratious *Mouth*, to *this
Mouth*: HIS waking *Eye*, to *this
Eye*: HIS powerfull *Hand* to *this
Hand*: then ſurely this fainted
Body

A Remedy
for want of
Money in the
remote cauſe
thereof.

Body will receiue *Breath* and *Life*, from the powerfull influence of so *Great a Maiestie,* and reuiue also the many other *fainting* Trades, that are *fallen* in it. The *Forreine Remote Causes,* I obserued to be the *Warres in Christendome,* or the *Trades* maintained with ready *Money Out of Christendome.* The former, either cause the *Exportation* of *Money,* as do the *Warres of Christians :* or hinder the *Importation* thereof, as doe the *Warres of Pirats.* A *Remedy* in the former of these I know none, besides that blessed disposition in H I s *Maiesty* to spare no *Cost* to make *Peace* : which hath made H I s *Fame* shine as farre as the Sunne shineth, and shall last as long as the Sunne and Moone endureth : and as sure as the Lord is faithfull, will be remembred on H I s *Posterity* for euer: Besides this I say, I know none, but *Patience* and *Prayer* : that *God* would

A Remedy of the Warres of Christians.

wou!d auert the heauy Iudgments
at this day on the Chriſtian world,
and giue vs grace to conſider *Our
peace*, in this *Our day* thereof. A
Remedy in the latter, may be either
by reducing of the ſtragling trade
of H I S *Maieſties* ſubiects into the
Dominions of the *King of Spaine*,
into *Gouernment* ; whereby they
alſo might goe in Fleetes, as other
gouerned Companies doe , and
the better defend themſelues a-
gainſt ſo *Common* and *Cruel* an eni-
my : or elſe by ſeeking reſtitution
of our wrongs in this kinde, where
it may be had : ſo farre as it may
concurre with the *Honour* of the
K I N G, to whoſe Great and Princes iudgement, I ſubmit the ſame.

The Remedy for the *Exportation
of Money* out of *Chriſtendome* by
the Trades before mentioned, dependeth much on the good Con-
cluſion hoped for , betweene the
Dutch and our *Nation*. Whereby
not

A Remedy
of diſorderly
Trade.

not only the *Indian Commodities*, which in thofe Trades are the principall, may be bought much better cheape, and confequently fpare a great deale of the *Treafure* now iffued out for the fame: but alfo, the *Natiue Commodities* of either Country, and as much as may bee of euery Country, may be brought into *Trade* and *Traine* with the *Indians*, and aduanced in their vfe and price: that fo at laft in ftead of Money for Wares, we may giue Wares for Wares according to the Law and nature of *Commerce*. And this good conclufion betweene the *Dutch* and *Vs*, is the rather to bee wifhed, and the more to be haftened, becaufe the fubtilty of the *Indians* is great, in taking aduantage of this vnhappy *Faction*, or rather *Fraction*, that is fallen betwixt vs. For thofe that haue trauelled the *Indies*, and obferued thofe people can tell, that the *Indians* doe

afcribe

aſcribe ſo much to the light of their vnderſtanding, that they doe account the reſt of the world blinde in Compariſon of them. Only they vouchſafe to the people of *Europe* this honour, to call them *One Eied men.* Which alſo *Maffeius* taketh notice of, in his Hiſtory of the *Indies*, that thoſe people dare beyond modeſty thus to brag; *Chinenſes duos habere oculos; Europæos vnum; & quod hominum eſt reliquum, cæcutire.* That the *Chineſes haue two Eies, the Europians one, and all the reſt of the people of the world are blinde.* And indeed they doe approoue themſelues to be *Quicke-ſighted* enough: for they are the *Antipodes* of *Chriſtians*, and are in ſcituation fartheſt remote from them, and yet can finde the *Meanes*, to pry into the *Mines* and *Treaſure* of the Chriſtian world. And therefore I ſay, it is high time that the *Dutch* and *We* left *Darting*

Ioan. Petr. Maffeius Hiſt. Ind. lib. 6.

I   at

at one another, and so ioine together, that as with one *Hand*, and
one *Heart*, and if they will needs
haue it so, *with that* one *Eie*, we
may collect and contract our sharp-
pest sence & sight into it; that as it is
said, some *Monoculists*, by the sharp-
nesse of the sence drawne to one
Eie, see better with that, then
both: we may at last put this remedy in practise, that we seem no longer blind men, to those *Indian* people. But herein on both parts, are
we humbly to implore HIS *Maiesties Regall Intercession*, that these
differences, betwixt the *Dutch* and
Vs, may no longer *Hang in sus-
pence*, but at last be drawne to that
happy and hopefull *Period* wee
haue so long looked & longed for.
That so the *Maiesty* of the KING,
arising like the *Glory* of the *Sun-ri-
sing* vpon this our *Horizon*, may di-
spell and disperse all the tempestuous
Mists and *Fogges*, that haue obscu-
red

red the same; and lend such a glorious *Light* and *Life* vnto this *Orbe* of ours, that *They* & *We*, like louers and friends fallen at oddes, may be redintegrated, renewed, and revnited, in vnfaigned *Amitie* and *Vnity*, that the name of *Hostilitie* betwixt *Them* and *Vs*, be neuer hereafter told in *Gath*, nor publish't in the streets of *Ashcalon*: And that the Publike complaints aswell of their * *Owne* people, as *Ours*, may no longer come vnder the view and censure of the world.

Another *Remedy* of this kinde, may bee H I S *Maiesties* gratious protection of the *Persian Trade* now so happily set on foote: that so neither the Enuy of any, at Home; nor the *Power or Policy* of any abroad, supplant vs in the same. Whereby the *Cloth* and *Tinne*, and other the *Natiue Commodities* of this *Kingdome*, may be brought into *Vse* and *Commerce* a-

I 2   mongst

* In a Translation out of a *Dutch* Copy, lately published in *Holland* by the *Dutch* themselues: in the face or Title wherof, these words are vsed : *That notwithstanding the extreme wrongs done by the* MAIORS *to the English Nation, Trading to the East Indies; yet it is the Iustice of God, they thriue not with it themselues.* Printed 26. *Iune.* 1622.

Another Remedy of the former kinde.

mongſt the *Perſians* alſo. Which
through Gods bleſſing, and his
Maieſties Royall Aſſiſtance, may be a
means to draw the whole Trade of
the *Perſian* ſilke into this *Kingdom,*
and make it the *Magazin* thereof,
for the ſupply of other Nations: to
the weakning of the *Turkes* power,
the increaſe of Trade in this *Common-wealth,* and with it H ɪ s *Maieſties* Cuſtomes, the Nauigation, and
employment of the poore: to the
Great Honour of the K ɪ ɴ ɢ, and
enriching of all H ɪ s *Kingdomes.*

And ſo much for the *Remedies*
about the *matter* of Trade in *Money,* the *Merchandize* followeth.
Which I conſidered *Iointly,* or *A-
part.* The things that hindred the
whole Trade, I noted to be *Deficient,* as the *want of Money,* or the
Eaſt India Stocke, which haue their
Remedy before: or *Efficient,* as *Vſury*
and *Litigious Suits of law,* to the *Remedies* whereof we now proceede.
The *Remedy* for *Vſury,* may   e

plenty of *Money.* For then, men
will haue no such cause to take *Money* at interest , as when *Money* is
scant. For as it is the scarcitie of
Money that maketh the high rates
of interest : so the plentie of *Money* will make the rates Low, better
then any Statute for that purpose. For although in the *Netherlands,* it is lawfull for a man to take
twenty in the hundred if he can
get it: (wherein it seemes the Author of the Tract against Vsury
was misinformed,) yet there, commonly money is let at 6. and 7. in
the hundred, by reason of the plenty of Money.

Or there is another Remedy for
Vsury, in giuing liberty to the subiects if so it may seeme good to His
Maiesties High Wisedome,) to buy
and sell , and to transport Billes of
debt from man to man : according
to the Custome of *Germany* and
the *LowCountries.* Which is found

Another Re-
medy for V-
sury.

I 3　　　to

to be an excellent meanes to fupply mens wants in courfe of trade; and tendeth alfo to the enlarging thereof. And for the *Extorfion* vpon the poore aboue noted: if a ftocke of Money were raifed in manner of a *Lumbard*, or otherwife in *London*, and in the *Countries* where much poore depend on Clothing; and elfe-where where there is caufe, whereby the multitudes of poore wherewith the *Kingdom* fwarmeth, might be from time to time fupplied for a fmall confideration; it would certainly giue great encouragement to the poore to labour, it would fet on worke many fatherleffe children that are ready to fterue, it would benefit the *Common-wealth* by their labours, and it would be an acceptable worke to *Almighty God*, fo to fupply their wants, and not to fuffer the faces of the poore to be ground by the extorfion of any.
And

And I am perſwaded, that euery good man would be willing, either to giue, or to lend, toward the raiſing of a ſtocke of *Money* for this purpoſe.

For *Litigious ſuits of Law*, if men beſtowed halfe that ſtudy and coſt in trade, which now adaies is ſpent in temerous and raſh ſuits of Law; ſurely the benefite that thence would ariſe to the *Common-wealth*, would equall or exceede in value, that which is ſpent in Law, which I thinke cannot be valued. The *Remedy* requireth great conſideration for ſuch is the Cauſe.

That the *ſuites of Law* in this *Kingdome* are now infinitely increaſt, to that they were in elder times, I thinke it is out of queſtion: The *Quære* is about the cauſe thereof. *Litigious ſuits of Law*, may ſeeme anciently to haue beene reſtrained, either by *Sureties*, or *Fines*, or both. *Of the Former* there is

Remedies for ligitious ſuits of Law.

I 4   yet

yet a defaced print in the Com-
mon-Pledges of *Doe and Roe*
Which were of old the names of
true and reall fureties, but are now
become formall only, and faigned
names of Courfe and Solemnity.
Whence alfo it is, that in ftead of
Reall fureties in *London*, faigned
fureties are deuifed from the dwelling of the party *Plaintife* : As for
example : if the plaintife dwell in
Cheape-fide : they enter for his
Sureties vpon the Record of
Court, *Iohn Cheape*, and *Richard
Side*. And in like manner where-
foeuer elfe the *Plaintife* dwelleth.

Of the Latter, to wit of *Fines*,
the vfe of them both in the *Kings
Bench,& Common-Pleas*,continueth
vnto this day. *In the Kings Bench*
the *Fines* are not fo ancient, for
thofe began in the 8 yeare of H1s
Maiefties Happy raigne ouer this
Kingdome : neither are they of like
value to thofe of the*Common-Pleas.*
Where-

Whereof His *Maieſtie* made then a *Graunt* to certaine *Patentees* for terme of yeares. But in the *Common-Pleas*, the *Fines* vpon *Originall Writs*, are held by the learned in the Law, to bee as ancient as the *Common-Law* it ſelfe.

Now whether the vſe of *Sureties*, or the Inſtitution of *Fines*, were inuented for the reſtraint of *Ligitious ſuits of Law* : or the Diſuſe and inequality of them, tendeth to the encreaſe thereof ; I humbly leaue that, to the wiſedome and iudgement of the *Reuerend Iudges*, and others learned in the Law : leaſt I ſeeme ὑπεροψονῖν παρ᾽ ὁ δ᾽ῖ φρονῖν. Neuertheleſſe there ſeemes to me, to be a print of them, in the Lawes and Cuſtomes of *Forreine Nations*. For which, if you pleaſe, let vs heare MAIMON a great RABBI. HEBRÆI, *litigioſum hominum genus*, ſaith he, *duplum rependere coegerunt, qui debitum ſcienter denegaret.*   Alſo

מורה
נבוכים
Maimon.lib.3.

Bodin. de Rep.
lib. 6.

Also F ɛ ꜱ ᴛ ᴠ ꜱ P ᴏ ᴍ ᴘ ᴇ ɪ ᴠ ꜱ,
cited by B ᴏ ᴅ ɪ ɴ. R ᴏ ᴍ ᴀ ɴ ɪ,
decimam partem eius rei, quæ in con-
trouersiam veniret in priuatis, aut
quintam in publicis iudicijs, impera-
bant. Ac licet Romani in Republica
libera, Vectigalia & tributa impera-
re sibi difficilimè paterentur, Vecti-
galia tamen Iudiciaria patienter tu-
lerunt.

In Part. iuris.
De Actionib.

Also H ᴏ ᴛ ᴛ ᴏ ᴍ ᴀ ɴ. R ᴏ ᴍ ᴀ-
ɴ ɪ *Sacramentum constituerunt, cer-*
tam viz. pecuniæ summam, vt qui
iudicio vicisset, suum sacramentū au-
ferret, victi autē ad ærarium rediret.

And lastly B ᴏ ᴅ ɪ ɴ. C ᴀ ʀ ᴏ-
ʟ ᴠ ꜱ ix. *Vectigal Iudiciarium ad*
cohibendam litigatorum hominum
indomitam atque effrenatam licen-
tiam imperauit. Quo vix vllum af-
flictis ærarij opibus vtilius, & Galliæ
Imperio litium innumerabili multi-
tudine oppresso, splendidius cogitari
poterat.

De Rep. lib. 6.

There is also in *France* an excellent

lent restraint of Law suits, by a *Law Merchant*, established in *Roan*, *Lions*, and *Tholosa* : whereby the other higher Courts of Iustice are eased of those Knotty questions that often fall out in matters of *Commerce*, which are harder to bee determined by the learned in the Law, and not so hard for Merchants and men of Trade.

Like to which, is that of the *Court of Conscience*, and the office for *Pollicies of Assurance* in London. The one granted by an Act of Parliament, in the 3. yeare of H I S *Maiesties* happy Raigne, the other by the Statute of 43. *Eliz.* And both are executed by *Merchants* and men of Trade : though in the latter the Statute ioineth certaine Ciuill and Common Lawyers with them in Commission, to assist them when there is cause : because such Assurances are grounded on the Ciuill Law. By which

which meanes H<small>IS</small> *Maiesties* other Courts of Iustice are eafed of the multiplicitie of Queſtions that might ariſe by ſuits of Law of this kinde.

And thus hauing been bold to make this ſhort relation of my poore obſeruation herein, I moſt humbly ſubmit this *Remedy* to the High wiſedome of H<small>IS</small> *Maieſtie*, to diſpoſe thereof in ſuch Manner and Meaſure, as the Nature and Number of the ſuits of Law, at this day in this Kingdome doe re-quire. In the reſtraint whereof H<small>IS</small> *Maieſtie* ſhall haue great *Honour* : H<small>IS</small> *Kingdome Peace* : the *Iudges Eaſe*: the *Subiects quietneſſe*, and the *Common-wealth* increaſe of *Trade*.

The Trades conſidered *apart*, I reduced to ſuch, as tend to the *Fortification of the Kingdome*, or *Maintenance of Trade*. The former I noted to be *Ordinance* or *Munition*.

In

Remedies for Ordinance.

In which case the *Philosopher* giueth good Counsell, Δεῖ φιλεῖν ὥσπερ μισήσοντα, μισεῖν δ᾽ ὥσπερ φιλήσοντα. *Sic amandum tanquam sis osurus , sic oportet odisse tanquam sis amaturus.*

Bias.

The latter I reduced to *Fishing* and *Clothing* , as the *Nurseries* of Trade. For the *Fishing,* the infinite treasure that Strangers search out of our Seas , the variety of Trade that thereby they purchase , the multitude of *Mariners* they breed, the Fleets of Shipping they maintaine, me thinkes should euery of them apart , or all of them together , be vnto vs as so many prouocations to rouze vs vp to the exercise thereof: Whereby H1s *Maiestie* might receiue such a Tolle or Custome of them, as other Princes doe in like case, and be once againe *Lord and Master* of the Seas, for all the dispute of the Author of *Mare liberum:* and the Natiue subiect encouraged by some Immunity or
Priuiledge,

The Remedy for Fishing.

Quæ non prosunt singula, multa iuvant. De remed.

Priuiledge, to lay hold on that benefit, which God and Nature hath
brought home to our doores.

For the *Clothing*, that alſo is a
point of *State* and *great conſequence*. The *Cauſes* of the decay
whereof, I obſerued to bee either
Domeſtique or *Forreine*. The *Domeſtique* ſome *paſt*, ſome *preſent*.
In which former, it may perhaps
ſeeme ſtrange, to ſpeake of a *Remedy* for a thing paſt. Wherein the
beſt Remedy I can thinke of, is, to
be warned by thoſe harmes, not to
diſturbe or diſtract Trade vpon
any ſuggeſtion, though neuer ſo
ſpecious. It is a ſafe rule, that in
*Rebus nouis conſtituendis euidens
eſſe debet vtilitas*. And in *Proiects*,
though they promiſe much, yet
the vtility is commonly *Contin-
gent*, which may be, or may not be.
But in the mutation of the naturall courſe of Trade, there ought
to be *Perſpicuity* and apparency of
euident

euident vtility : Elſe a *Breach* may
be ſooner made in Trade then can
be *repaired* : and the *Current* once
diuerted, will hardly bee *reuolued*,
into it genuine *Source* and *Courſe* a-
gaine.

The *preſent Domeſtique Cauſes*
of the Decay of *Clothing*, I conſidered in the Trade vnder the *Clothier*, or vnder the *Merchant*. Vnder the *Clothier*, I noted the *Ill making* and *Falſe ſealing* of Cloth :
and both through the *Non-execution* of the Statute of 4. of the KING.
The abuſe wherof is growne to be
very great, and the reformation
hath beene by HIs *Maieſties* Proclamations and otherwiſe, ſo much
and ſo oft attempted of late yeares,
and nothing therein effected, that it
ſeemeth a very difficult matter to
reforme the ſame. Neuertheleſſe
if it may pleaſe HIS *Maieſtie*, to
commit the care of the execution
of the Statute, to ſome of the Principall

The Remedy
for Clothing.

The Remedy for Clothing.

cipall Cities and Townes in the Clothing Counties, where Broad Clothes, Kerfies, and Perpetuanoes are made; and to make them the *Ouerseers* mentioned in the Statute, inftead of thofe ignorant and negligent Searchers, with reafonable allowance for their paines; I am confident it would proue a finguler Remedy. For we haue not only the example of the *Low Countries,* where this courfe is taken, but

Examples of *Worcester, Colchefter,* and *Canterbury*.

alfo here with vs: as *Worcefter* for that fort of Clothes, *Colchefter* for Bayes, and *Canterbury* for Sayes. In all which places the former abufes are remoued by this means; and the Clothes, and Bayes, and Manufactures of thofe Cities, triumph in great credit and eftimation. Which execution of the faide Statute, is the rather to be committed to the care and charge of the principall Cities and Townes in the Clothing Counties; becaufe

by

by ancient Statutes not repealed, all Clothes and Kersies ought to bee brought to the next City, Borough, or Towne Corporate, to be sealed, before they be put to sale. And if such Clothes so sealed, proue defectiue, that Corporation or Towneship that so hath sealed them, shall forfeit the whole value thereof.

The reformation of which abuse will redound to the benefit of the *Clothier*, as well as the *Merchant*. For none is more hurt with false Cloth, then that Clothier which maketh true Cloth: because his markets are alwayes hurt by the cheapnesse that false Cloth may be afforded at. Therefore to facilitate this Remedy, I haue made a collection of all the principall Cities and Townes in the Clothing Counties for this purpose, as by a list thereof, fixed to the end of this discourse may appeare, that so a

K   worke

4. & 5. P. & M 5.

A Remedy
for the ex-
portation of
Wools.

worke of this nature be no longer
deferred , wherein the *Honour of
the* K I N G, and the *Benefit* of the
Publique are so much inuolued.

Vnder the *Merchant* I obserued
the Cloth-Trade to suffer at *Home*
and *Abroad* : At *Home*, either by
exporting the *Materials* of Clothing,or by Ore-lading the Cloth-
Trade with charge. The Remedy
in the former, were to lay a restraint of exportation of Wools
and Wool-fels out of *Ireland*, and
to quicken the execution of the
Statute for that purpose in
England, by encouraging the dis-
couerers of such abuses.

The latter is the Sur-charging of
the Cloth Trade, either generally
or specially : this last, in the Im-
positions and Imprest monies im-
posed by the *Merchant Aduenturers*: which as it is a charge laid vpon the *Drapery* of the *Kingdome*, I
conceiue, vnder fauour, is a matter
that

that trencheth into the Supreme power and dignity of the K I N G, and is peculiar to H I M alone. And if for *Gouernment*, or other iuſt cauſes in *Societies* and *Corporations*, there be a neceſſity of paying of debts, or defraying of neceſſary charge ; I ſhould thinke it better policy to ſpare the *Cloth*, and other the *Natiue Commodities* of the *Kingdom*, and to implore H I s *Maieſties* fauour, to leuy ſuch charge vpon the *Forreine Commodities* : according to the Counſell of *Stephanus*, *Si Vectigal nouum euitari non poteſt, tunc onerentur merces perigrinæ, quæ ad luxum magis quàm ad neceſſitatem faciunt.* And this I conceiue would be a good remedy for eaſing the Cloth Trade of the preſent charge vnder the Merchants : which would alſo bee a meanes for paying of their debts, with a little more length of time, and a great deale of encourage-

K 2 ment,

A Remedy for the charge vpon the Cloth.

Stephan lib. Senten.

ment, both to Clothiers and Merchants in the Cloth Trade.

And *Abroad*, if it appeare vpon examination, that the Residence of the Merchant Aduenturers at *Delft* in *Holland* be inconuenient for the Trade: As H I s *Maieſtie* was gracioufly pleafed to giue them that liberty for a tryall, fo it may pleafe H I s *Maieſtie* to difpofe thereof, in fome more fit place for their's and the *Publique good*.

The *Forreine Cauſes* of the Decay of the *Drapery*, I noted to bee *Generall*, as the *Warres*; or *Speciall*, as the great *Impoſition in Holland*. The one is the worke of *God*, the other of the K I N G, to remoue the fame. To whom I recommend them both.

A Remedy for Monopolies and too ftrict Trade.

And thus farre for the *Remedies* in the *Matter of Trade*, confidered in *Money* and *Merchandize*: the *Forme* followeth in *Gouerned* and *Vngouerned Trade*. In the *Former*

I

I obſerued a *too ſtrict* , and in the *latter* a *too looſe* forme of Trade. The *Remedy* in the One, if it ſeeme good to the high wiſedome of HIS *Maieſtie*, may be *Priuatiue* , in racing and rooting out the name and vſe of *Monopolies* from a-mongſt this Nation, as HIS *Maie-ſtie* hath royally begun in that HIS Gracious Proclamation before mentioned. And to free and open the courſe of Trade, where now it is vnequally ſtopt, to the encou-ragement of the ſubiects, and the benefit of the Publique.

In the other *Poſitiue*, by diſpo-ſing the Trades of HIS *Maieſties* ſubiects that are now diſtracted; in-to *Order* and *Gouernment*. Where-of none hath more need , as hath been ſhewed, then thoſe that Trade into the Dominions of the *King of Spaine.* Whoſe Trade the rather calleth for redreſſe , becauſe it ex-porteth Cloth and other the Ma-

K 3 nufactures

A Remedy for too looſe Trade.

nufactures of the *Kingdome*, and importeth *Treasure*, the life of Trade : In both which there is now a maruellous great defect, and Trade in all mens hands *become so poore and leane*, that it doth scarce, *hærere offibus*. For where *Trade* is *disordred*, and the *Traders vngouerned*, there they are like a house deuided , which cannot long subsist : according to that of the Orator, *Nec domus vlla, nec Ciuitas, nec Societas, nec Gens, nec hominum vniuersum genus stare, nec rerum natura omnis , nec sine imperio mundus ipse potest.*

Cic. de Legib.

μόνῳ σοφῷ Θεῷ δόξα.

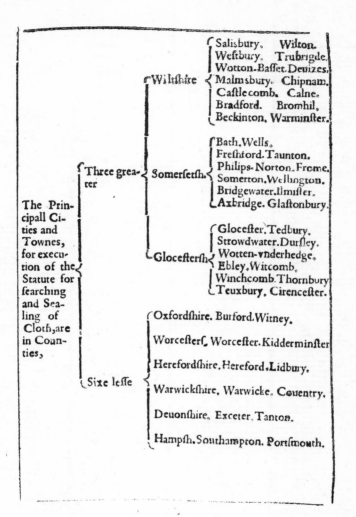

The Principall Cities and Townes, for execution of the Statute for searching and Sealing of Cloth, are in Counties,

Three greater

- **Wiltshire** — Salisbury. Wilton. Westbury. Trubrigde. Wotton-Basset. Deuizes. Malmsbury. Chipnam. Castlecomb. Calne. Bradford. Bromhil. Beckinton. Warminster.

- **Somersetsh.** — Bath. Wells. Freshford. Taunton. Philips-Norton. Frome. Somerton. Wellington. Bridgewater. Ilmister. Axbridge. Glastonbury.

- **Glocestersh.** — Glocester. Tedbury. Strowdwater. Dursley. Wotten-vnderhedge. Ebley. Witcomb. Winchcomb. Thornbury. Teuxbury. Cirencester.

Sixe lesse

- Oxfordshire. Burford. Witney.
- Worcesters. Worcester. Kidderminster.
- Herefordshire. Hereford. Lidbury.
- Warwickshire. Warwicke. Couentry.
- Deuonshire. Exceter. Tanton.
- Hampsh. Southampton. Portsmouth.